Poems on the Underground

POEMS ON THE UNDERGROUND

EDITED BY
GERARD BENSON
JUDITH CHERNAIK
CICELY HERBERT

PENGUIN BOOKS

PENGUIN BOOKS

UK | USA | Canada | Ireland | Australia
India | New Zealand | South Africa

Penguin Books is part of the Penguin Random House
group of companies whose addresses can be found at
global.penguinrandomhouse.com.

Penguin
Random House
UK

First published in Particular Books 2012
This edition published in Penguin Books 2015

006

Poems set in Gill Sans Mt Std
Headings set in P22 Johnston Underground
Text face and footnotes set in Adobe Caslon Pro
Typeset by Penguin Books UK
Printed in Great Britain by Clays Ltd, Elcograf S.p.A.

A CIP catalogue record for this book is available from the
British Library

ISBN: 978-0-141-38954-7

www.greenpenguin.co.uk

MIX
Paper from
responsible sources
FSC® C018179

Penguin Random House is committed to a
sustainable future for our business, our readers
and our planet. This book is made from Forest
Stewardship Council® certified paper.

'There is a man haunts the forest, that hangs odes upon hawthorns, and elegies on brambles . . .'

Shakespeare, *As You Like It*, Act 3, Scene 2

To the farsighted managers of London Underground, who have kept poems circling on Tube trains for the past thirty years; and to the poets past and present whose words have entertained millions on their Underground journeys.

The Editors

Contents

London

The Wider World

Exile and Loss

The Natural World

The Darker Side

The Artist as 'Maker'

The Poet as Prophet

**Poetry:
A Defence**

Foreword

Poems on the Underground started life in January 1986 as an experiment by three friends, lovers of poetry, who persuaded London Underground to post a few poems in its trains. The Tube managers kindly doubled the number of spaces for which we secured funding, and London Underground has supported the programme ever since.

We had a few precedents, going back to the love-sick Orlando, in Shakespeare's *As You Like It*, hanging 'odes upon hawthorns, and elegies on brambles', to the scorn of his beloved Rosalind. Verses about the Thames were inscribed in the pavement between Westminster and Waterloo Bridges for the 1951 Festival of Britain; the short poems, long since vandalized and removed, were by an eclectic band of poets including Blake, T. S. Eliot and Spike Milligan.

Right from the start, our own project struck a special chord with the public. Poets and press thronged the launch at Aldwych Station, on the Strand – also a victim of changing times (it was shut in 1994). Since then, the simple idea of offering poetry to a mass audience on public transport has spread to cities across the world, from Dublin, Paris, Stuttgart, Helsinki, Stockholm, Vienna and Madrid to Prague, Warsaw, Moscow, Melbourne, Shanghai and Beijing. Our posters too travel widely, going to British Council teaching centres in Europe, Asia and Africa as well as schools and libraries throughout the UK.

We've also expanded beyond the Tube, commissioning new poems for *Carnival of the Animals* (the poets carefully chosen for their resemblance to each animal) and new music for a variety of poems old and new. We've regularly offered live events related to the Tube displays, combining music, poetry and occasionally film. We've organized several competitions for young poets, working with the Poetry Society; the prize was display on the Tube. We also ran a competition for over-eighteens with *The Times Literary Supplement* and we've commissioned new English translations of French, German and Finnish classic and contemporary poems.

Our first display of poems featured Seamus Heaney (nearly a decade before he won the Nobel Prize for Literature), the young Guyanese writer Grace Nichols, Shelley, Robert Burns and the American poet William Carlos Williams, all of whom hoped to reach a general public with poetry that was revolutionary for its time. The combination of old and new, familiar and unfamiliar, seemed to work, and we've held all along to the same general principles: to support living poets; to pay tribute to the magnificent tradition of English poetry; and to include many less-famous poets who have contributed to the richness and diversity of that tradition.

In this anthology, the poems that have been displayed on London Underground trains are collected together under headings which embrace the great subjects of human existence: love, death, music and art, dreams, the natural world, war and peace. We have been intrigued to discover how the poems, placed together in this way, often seem to find an extra depth through their proximity to one another. One poem seems to enrich another and so leads the reader on a journey full of discoveries, odd paths and byways, or across oceans to other lands, and indeed to other worlds.

All the poems reprinted here have appeared as posters on London Underground trains, and have been read by thousands of commuters and visitors from every part of the globe. There are poems that have been written as a result of the darkest human experiences, including war, exile and death, while other poems reflect on joyous and life-enhancing moments: the birth of a child, love of one's home or country, the profound pleasures of great art or beauty.

Perhaps it is through reading some of these poems that a person might be enabled to find a way through Dante's 'dark wood'. But if that is too great a claim, we can at least share with the poets their gift for transforming our memories, fears and delights into words that will continue to bring pleasure for generations to come.

Our project remains possible through the generous support of London Underground and Transport for London. We have also been fortunate in securing support from Arts Council England and the British Council, which distributes the poems around the world and is responsible for several 'exchanges' of poems, for instance with Helsinki and Oslo, Paris, Porto, Shanghai and New York. We also work closely with the Poetry Society and the Poetry Book Society, which are so active in promoting poetry to young people and to the wider world. We owe a special debt to Tom Davidson, whose elegant designs for the Tube posters have contributed immeasurably to their popularity. To all, our thanks.

Gerard Benson, Judith Chernaik,
Cicely Herbert
London, 2012

Our dear friend and colleague Gerard Benson died in April 2014. His many talents contributed immeasurably to the broad reach of *Poems on the Underground*. He combined a profound knowledge of literature with a love of comic poetry, riddles, and nonsense poems, and he had an unerring instinct for choosing poems with broad appeal. He knew exactly what would work on the Tube. He added an anarchic strain to our selections, and his readings at live events, including his riveting declamation of Edwin Morgan's 'Loch Ness Monster's Song', enchanted audiences in London and, on one memorable occasion, at New York's Grand Central Station. His voice lives on in a recording of his poems for the Poetry Archive, his ten poetry collections and his award-winning *Puffin* anthologies.

JC and CH
London, 2015

Love

'Because I love you more than I can say'

Two Fragments

Love holds me captive again
and I tremble with bittersweet longing

As a gale on the mountainside bends the oak tree
I am rocked by my love

Sappho
Translated by Cicely Herbert

Longings

Like the beautiful bodies of those who died before growing old,
sadly shut away in a sumptuous mausoleum,
roses by the head, Jasmine at the feet –
so appear the longings that have passed
without being satisfied, not one of them granted
a single night of pleasure, or one of its radiant mornings.

C. P. Cavafy

Love Without Hope

Love without hope, as when the young bird-catcher
Swept off his tall hat to the Squire's own daughter,
So let the imprisoned larks escape and fly
Singing about her head, as she rode by.

Robert Graves

Her Anxiety

Earth in beauty dressed
Awaits returning spring.
All true love must die,
Alter at the best
Into some lesser thing.
Prove that I lie.

Such body lovers have,
Such exacting breath,
That they touch or sigh.
Every touch they give,
Love is nearer death.
Prove that I lie.

What He Said

What could my mother be
to yours? What kin is my father
to yours anyway? And how
did you and I meet ever?
                    But in love
our hearts have mingled
like red earth and pouring rain.

Cempulappeyanirar
Translated by A. K. Ramanujan

The Good Morrow

I wonder, by my troth, what thou and I
Did, till we loved; were we not weaned till then,
But sucked on country pleasures, childishly?
Or snorted we in the Seven Sleepers' den?
'Twas so; but this, all pleasures fancies be.
If ever any beauty I did see,
Which I desired, and got, 'twas but a dream of thee.

And now good morrow to our waking souls,
Which watch not one another out of fear;
For love, all love of other sights controls,
And makes one little room, an everywhere.
Let sea-discoverers to new worlds have gone,
Let maps to others, worlds on worlds have shown,
Let us possess one world; each hath one, and is one.

My face in thine eye, thine in mine appears,
And true plain hearts do in the faces rest;
Where can we find two better hemispheres,
Without sharp North, without declining West?
Whatever dies, was not mixed equally;
If our two loves be one; or thou and I
Love so alike that none do slacken, none
   can die.

Separation

Your absence has gone through me
Like thread through a needle.
Everything I do is stitched with its colour.

W. S. Merwin

'What lips my lips have kissed, and where, and why'

What lips my lips have kissed, and where, and why,
I have forgotten, and what arms have lain
Under my head till morning; but the rain
Is full of ghosts tonight, that tap and sigh
Upon the glass and listen for reply,
And in my heart there stirs a quiet pain
For unremembered lads that not again
Will turn to me at midnight with a cry.
Thus in the winter stands the lonely tree,
Nor knows what birds have vanished one by one,
Yet knows its boughs more silent than before:
I cannot say what loves have come and gone,
I only know that summer sang in me
A little while, that in me sings no more.

They Flee from Me

They flee from me that sometime did me seek
With naked foot stalking in my chamber.
I have seen them gentle, tame, and meek
That now are wild, and do not remember
That sometime they put themselves in danger
To take bread at my hand, and now they range,
Busily seeking with a continual change.

Thanked be fortune it hath been otherwise
Twenty times better, but once in special,
In thin array after a pleasant guise
When her loose gown from her shoulders did fall
And she me caught in her arms long and small,
Therewithal sweetly did me kiss
And softly said, Dear heart, how like you this?

It was no dream, I lay broad waking.
But all is turned through my gentleness
Into a strange fashion of forsaking,
And I have leave to go of her goodness,
And she also to use newfangleness.
But since that I so kindly am served,
I would fain know what she hath deserved.

Sir Thomas Wyatt

The Sick Rose

O Rose thou art sick.
The invisible worm
That flies in the night
In the howling storm,

Has found out thy bed
Of crimson joy:
And his dark secret love
Does thy life destroy.

'So we'll go no more a-roving'

So we'll go no more a-roving
  So late into the night,
Though the heart be still as loving,
  And the moon be still as bright.

For the sword outwears its sheath,
  And the soul wears out the breast,
And the heart must pause to breathe,
  And Love itself have rest.

Though the night was made for loving,
  And the day returns too soon,
Yet we'll go no more a-roving
  By the light of the moon.

George Gordon, Lord Byron

If I Could Tell You

Time will say nothing but I told you so,
Time only knows the price we have to pay;
If I could tell you I would let you know.

If we should weep when clowns put on their
    show,
If we should stumble when musicians play,
Time will say nothing but I told you so.

There are no fortunes to be told, although,
Because I love you more than I can say,
If I could tell you I would let you know.

The winds must come from somewhere when
    they blow,
There must be reasons why the leaves decay;
Time will say nothing but I told you so.

Perhaps the roses really want to grow,
The vision seriously intends to stay;
If I could tell you I would let you know.

Suppose the lions all get up and go,
And all the brooks and soldiers run away;
Will Time say nothing but I told you so?
If I could tell you I would let you know.

Celia Celia

When I am sad and weary
When I think all hope has gone
When I walk along High Holborn
I think of you with nothing on

Adrian Mitchell

Animals

Have you forgotten what we were like then
when we were still first rate
and the day came fat with an apple in its mouth

it's no use worrying about Time
but we did have a few tricks up our sleeves
and turned some sharp corners

the whole pasture looked like our meal
we didn't need speedometers
we could manage cocktails out of ice and water

I wouldn't want to be faster
or greener than now if you were with me O you
were the best of all my days

'Since there's no help, come let us kiss and part'

Since there's no help, come let us kiss and part,
Nay, I have done: you get no more of me,
And I am glad, yea glad with all my heart
That thus so cleanly I myself can free,
Shake hands for ever, cancel all our vows,
And when we meet at any time again,
Be it not seen in either of our brows
That we one jot of former love retain.
Now at the last gasp of love's latest breath,
When his pulse failing, passion speechless lies,
When faith is kneeling by his bed of death,
And innocence is closing up his eyes,
  Now if thou wouldst, when all have given him over,
  From death to life thou might'st him yet recover.

Michael Drayton

One Art

The art of losing isn't hard to master;
so many things seem filled with the intent
to be lost that their loss is no disaster.

Lose something every day. Accept the fluster
of lost door keys, the hour badly spent.
The art of losing isn't hard to master.

Then practice losing farther, losing faster:
places, and names, and where it was you
    meant
to travel. None of these will bring disaster.

I lost my mother's watch. And look! my last, or
next-to-last, of three loved houses went.
The art of losing isn't hard to master.

I lost two cities, lovely ones. And, vaster,
some realms I owned, two rivers, a continent.
I miss them, but it wasn't a disaster.

— Even losing you (the joking voice, a gesture
I love) I shan't have lied. It's evident
the art of losing's not too hard to master
though it may look like (*Write* it!) like disaster.

Content

Like walking in fog, in fog and mud,
do you remember, love? We kept,
for once, to the tourist path, boxed in mist,
conscious of just our feet and breath,
and at the peak, sat hand in hand, and let
the cliffs we'd climbed and cliffs to come
reveal themselves and be veiled again
quietly, with the prevailing wind.

Kate Clanchy

'Western wind when wilt thou blow'

Western wind when wilt thou blow
the small rain down can rain
Christ that my love were in my arms
and I in my bed again

London

'Earth has not anything to show more fair'

Composed upon Westminster Bridge, September 3, 1802

Earth has not anything to show more fair:
Dull would he be of soul who could pass by
A sight so touching in its majesty:
This City now doth like a garment wear
The beauty of the morning; silent, bare,
Ships, towers, domes, theatres, and
   temples lie
Open unto the fields, and to the sky;
All bright and glittering in the smokeless air.
Never did sun more beautifully steep
In his first splendour valley, rock, or hill;
Ne'er saw I, never felt, a calm so deep!
The river glideth at his own sweet will:
Dear God! the very houses seem asleep;
And all that mighty heart is lying still!

William Wordsworth

Toussaint L'Ouverture Acknowledges Wordsworth's Sonnet 'To Toussaint L'Ouverture'

I have never walked on Westminster Bridge
or had a close-up view of daffodils.
My childhood's roots are the Haitian hills
where runaway slaves made a freedom
   pledge
and scarlet poincianas flaunt their scent.
I have never walked on Westminster Bridge
or speak, like you, with Cumbrian accent.
My tongue bridges Europe to Dahomey.

Yet how sweet is the smell of liberty
when human beings share a common garment.
So, thanks brother, for your sonnet's tribute.
May it resound when the Thames' text stays mute.
And what better ground than a city's bridge
for my unchained ghost to trumpet love's decree.

'Tagus farewell'

Tagus farewell, that westward with thy streams
Turns up the grains of gold already tried:
With spur and sail for I go seek the Thames
Gainward the sun that showeth her wealthy pride
And to the town which Brutus sought by dreams
Like bended moon doth lend her lusty side.
My king, my country, alone for whom I live,
Of mighty love the wings for this me give.

Sir Thomas Wyatt

Tagus: The Spanish and Portuguese river famous for its gold. Wyatt, Ambassador to Spain, had been recalled to England by Henry VIII.
Brutus: A descendant of Aeneas, who dreamed that he was destined to found a kingdom in Albion.

Symphony in Yellow

An omnibus across the bridge
   Crawls like a yellow butterfly,
   And, here and there, a passer-by
Shows like a little restless midge.

Big barges full of yellow hay
   Are moored against the shadowy wharf,
   And, like a yellow silken scarf,
The thick fog hangs along the quay.

The yellow leaves begin to fade
   And flutter from the Temple elms,
   And at my feet the pale green Thames
Lies like a rod of rippled jade.

Oscar Wilde

In the Heart of Hackney

for Aidan Andrew Dun

Behold, a swan. Ten houseboats on the Lee.
  A cyclist on the towpath. Gentle rain.
A pigeon in a white apple-blossoming tree.
  And through the Marsh the rumble of a train.

Two courting geese waddle on the bank
  Croaking. A man unties his boat.
Police cars howl and whoop. And vast and blank
  The rain cloud of the sky is trampled underfoot.

Behold, a dove. And in Bomb Crater Pond
  Fat frogs ignore the rain.
Each trembling rush signals like a wand
  Earthing the magic of London once again.

In the heart of Hackney, five miles from Kentish Town,
By Lammas Lands the reed beds are glowing rich and brown.

Sebastian Barker

Immigrant

November '63: eight months in London.
I pause on the low bridge to watch the pelicans:
they float swanlike, arching their white necks
over only slightly ruffled bundles of wings,
burying awkward beaks in the lake's water.

I clench cold fists in my Marks and Spencer's jacket
and secretly test my accent once again:
St James's Park; St James's Park; St James's Park.

Ballad of the Londoner

Evening falls on the smoky walls,
   And the railings drip with rain,
And I will cross the old river
   To see my girl again.

The great and solemn-gliding tram,
   Love's still-mysterious car,
Has many a light of gold and white,
   And a single dark red star.

I know a garden in a street
   Which no one ever knew;
I know a rose beyond the Thames,
   Where flowers are pale and few.

James Elroy Flecker

The Embankment

(The Fantasia of a Fallen Gentleman on a Cold, Bitter Night)

Once, in finesse of fiddles found I ecstasy,
In a flash of gold heels on the hard pavement.
Now see I
That warmth's the very stuff of poesy.
Oh, God, make small
The old star-eaten blanket of the sky,
That I may fold it round me and in comfort lie.

London Bells

Two sticks and an apple,
Ring the bells at Whitechapel.

Old Father Bald Pate,
Ring the bells at Aldgate.

Maids in white aprons,
Ring the bells at St Catherine's.

Oranges and lemons,
Ring the bells at St Clement's.

When will you pay me?
Ring the bells at the Old Bailey.

When I am rich,
Ring the bells at Fleetditch.

When will that be?
Ring the bells at Stepney.

When I am old,
Ring the great bell at Paul's.

Anon.

City

When the great bell
BOOMS over the Portland stone urn, and
From the carved cedar wood
Rises the odour of incense,
I SIT DOWN
In St Botolph Bishopsgate Churchyard
And wait for the spirit of my grandfather
Toddling along from the Barbican.

Poem on the Underground

Proud readers
Hide behind tall newspapers.

The young are all arms and legs
Knackered by youth.

Tourists sit bolt upright
Trusting in nothing.

Only the drunk and the crazy
Aspire to converse.

Only the poet
Peruses his poem among the adverts.

Only the elderly person
Observes the request that the seat be offered to an elderly person.

D. J. Enright

Monopoly

We sat like slum landlords around the board
buying each other out with fake banknotes,
until we lost more than we could afford,
or ever hope to pay back. Now our seats
are empty – one by one we left the game
to play for real, at first completely lost
in this other world, its building sites, its rain;
but slowly learned the rules or made our own,
stayed out of jail and kept our noses clean.
And now there's only me – sole freeholder
of every empty office space in town,
and from the quayside I can count the cost
each low tide brings – the skeletons and rust
of boats, cars, hats, boots, iron, a terrier.

from To the City of London

London, thou art of towns *A per se.*
   Sovereign of cities, seemliest in sight,
Of high renown, riches, and royalty;
   Of lords, barons, and many a goodly knight;
   Of most delectable lusty ladies bright;
Of famous prelates in habits clerical;
   Of merchants full of substance and might:
London, thou art the flower of cities all . . .

Above all rivers thy river hath renown,
   Whose beryl streams, pleasant and preclare,
Under thy lusty walls runneth down;
   Where many a swan doth swim with wings fair;
   Where many a barge doth sail, and row with oar,
Where many a ship doth rest with top-royal.
   O! town of towns, patron and not-compare:
London, thou art the flower of cities all . . .

Strong be thy walls that about thee stands;
   Wise be the people that within thee dwells;
Fresh is thy river with his lusty strands;
   Blithe be thy churches, well sounding be thy bells;
   Rich be thy merchants in substance that excels;
Fair be thy wives, right lovesome, white and small;
   Clear be thy virgins, lusty under kells:
London, thou art the flower of cities all.

The Wider World

'My soul has grown deep like the rivers'

Ibadan

Ibadan,
     running splash of rust
and gold – flung and scattered
among seven hills like broken
china in the sun.

J. P. Clark-Bekederemo

Belgrade

White bone among the clouds

You arise out of your pyre
Out of your ploughed-up barrows
Out of your scattered ashes

You arise out of your disappearance

The sun keeps you
In its golden reliquary
High above the yapping of centuries

And bears you to the marriage
Of the fourth river of Paradise
With the thirty-sixth river of Earth

White bone among the clouds
Bone of our bones

Vasko Popa
Translated by Anne Pennington

Baku at Night

Reaching down to the starless heavy sea
in the pitch-black night,
Baku is a sunny wheatfield.
High above on a hill,
grains of light hit my face by the handfuls,
and the music in the air flows like the Bosporus.
High above on a hill,
my heart goes out like a raft
                into the endless absence,
                beyond memory
                down to the starless heavy sea
                in the pitch dark.

Nazim Hikmet
Translated by Randy Blasing and Mutlu Konuk

Star

I returned to you years later,
gray and lovely city,
unchanging city
buried in the waters of the past.

I'm no longer the student
of philosophy, poetry, and curiosity,
I'm not the young poet who wrote
too many lines

and wandered in the maze
of narrow streets and illusions.
The sovereign of clocks and shadows
has touched my brow with his hand,

but still I'm guided by
a star by brightness
and only brightness
can undo or save me.

Adam Zagajewski
Translated by Clare Cavanagh

J. P. Donleavy's Dublin

'When you stop to consider
The days spent dreaming of a future
And say then, that was my life.'

For the days are long –
From the first milk van
To the last shout in the night,
An eternity. But the weeks go by
Like birds; and the years, the years
Fly past anti-clockwise
Like clock hands in a bar mirror.

Derek Mahon

Thanks Forever

Look at those empty ships
floating north
between south-running ice
like big tulips
in the Narrows
under the Verrazano
toward the city harbor.
I'm parked here,
out of work all year.

No hurry now
and sleep badly.
But I'm self-employed.
My new job's
to wave them in.
Hello freighter,
hello tanker.
Welcome, welcome,
to New York.

Listening to a Monk from Shu Playing the Lute

The monk from Shu with his green lute-case walked
Westward down Emei Shan, and at the sound
Of the first notes he strummed for me I heard
A thousand valleys' rustling pines resound.
My heart was cleansed, as if in flowing water.
In bells of frost I heard the resonance die.
Dusk came unnoticed over the emerald hills
And autumn clouds layered the darkening sky.

Li Bai
Translated by Vikram Seth

Finding India in Unexpected Places

A street in Bath,
    a bus in Medellín,
a gesture in Gyeongju—

A yellow fragrance in Oaxaca,
  Oleanders
    on the isle of Skopelos—

Memories distort geography.

But how did the Mayas
    learn about elephants,
  about Ganesh, and the precise shape
    of his ears?

Two Poems
Written at
Maple Bridge
Near Su-Chou

Maple Bridge Night Mooring

Moon set, a crow caws,
    frost fills the sky
River, maple, fishing-fires
    cross my troubled sleep.
Beyond the walls of Su-chou
    from Cold Mountain temple
The midnight bell sounds
    reach my boat.

written c. AD 765

Chang Chi
Translated by Gary Snyder

At Maple Bridge

Men are mixing gravel and cement
At Maple bridge,
Down an alley by a tea-stall
From Cold Mountain temple;
Where Chang Chi heard the bell.
The stone step moorage
Empty, lapping water,
And the bell sound has travelled
Far across the sea.

written AD 1984

The Palm Trees at Chigawe

You stood like women in green
Proud travellers in panama hats and java print
Your fruit-milk caused monkeys and shepherds to scramble
Your dry leaves were banners for night fishermen
But now stunted trees stand still beheaded—
A curious sight for the tourists.

Jack Mapanje

Inside My Zulu Hut

It is a hive
without any bees
to build the walls
with golden bricks of honey.
A cave cluttered
with a millstone,
calabashes of sour milk
claypots of foaming beer
sleeping grass mats
wooden head rests
tanned goat skins
tied with *riempies*
to wattle rafters
blackened by the smoke
of kneaded cow dung
burning under
the three-legged pot
on the earthen floor
to cook my porridge.

Riempies: Dried strips of hide.

Nocturne

And we shall bathe, my love, in the presence of Africa.
Furnishings from Guinea and the Congo, heavy and burnished, calm and dark.
Masks, pure and primeval, on the walls, distant but so present!
Ebony thrones for ancestral guests, the Princes of the hill country.
Musky perfumes, thick grass-mats of silence,
Shadowed cushions for leisure, the sound of a spring – of peace.
Mythic language; and far-off songs, voices woven like the strip-cloths of the Sudan.
And then, dear lamp, your kindness in cradling the obsession with this presence,
Black, white, and red: oh! red like the earth of Africa.

Léopold Sédar Senghor
Translated by Gerard Benson

The Negro Speaks of Rivers

I've known rivers:
I've known rivers ancient as the world and older than the flow of human blood in human veins.

My soul has grown deep like the rivers.

I bathed in the Euphrates when dawns were young.
I built my hut near the Congo and it lulled me to sleep.
I looked upon the Nile and raised the pyramids above it.
I heard the singing of the Mississippi when Abe Lincoln went down to New Orleans, and I've seen
  its muddy bosom turn all golden in the sunset.

I've known rivers:
Ancient, dusky rivers.

My soul has grown deep like the rivers.

Exile and Loss
'All the old songs'

My Voice

I come from a distant land
with a foreign knapsack on my back
with a silenced song on my lips

As I travelled down the river of my life
I saw my voice
(like Jonah)
swallowed by a whale

And my very life lived in my voice
Kabul, December 1989

Partaw Naderi
Translated by Sarah Maguire and Yama Yari

The Exiles

The many ships that left our country
with white wings for Canada.
They are like handkerchiefs in our memories
and the brine like tears
and in their masts sailors singing
like birds on branches.
That sea of May running in such blue,
a moon at night, a sun at daytime,
and the moon like a yellow fruit,
like a plate on a wall
to which they raise their hands
like a silver magnet
with piercing rays
streaming into the heart.

Iain Crichton Smith

The Emigrant Irish

Like oil lamps we put them out the back,

of our houses, of our minds. We had lights
better than, newer than and then

a time came, this time and now
we need them. Their dread, makeshift example.

They would have thrived on our necessities.
What they survived we could not even live.
By their lights now it is time to
imagine how they stood there, what they stood with,
that their possessions may become our power.

Cardboard. Iron. Their hardships parcelled in them.
Patience. Fortitude. Long-suffering
in the bruise-coloured dusk of the New World.

And all the old songs. And nothing to lose.

Eavan Boland

Indian Cooking

The bottom of the pan was a palette—
paprika, cayenne, dhania
haldi, heaped like powder-paints.

Melted ghee made lakes, golden rivers.
The keema frying, my mother waited
for the fat to bubble to the surface.

Friends brought silver-leaf.
I dropped it on khir—
special rice pudding for parties.

I tasted the landscape, customs
of my father's country—
its fever on biting a chilli.

'Into my heart an air that kills'

Into my heart an air that kills
   From yon far country blows:
What are those blue remembered hills,
   What spires, what farms are those?

That is the land of lost content,
   I see it shining plain,
The happy highways where I went
   And cannot come again.

A. E. Housman

A Private Life

I want to drive home in the dusk
of some late afternoon,

the journey slow, the tractors spilling hay,
the land immense and bright, like memory,

the pit towns smudges of graphite,
their names scratched out for good:
    Lumphinnans;

Kelty. I want to see
the darkened rooms, the cups and wireless
    sets,

the crimson lamps across the playing fields,
the soft men walking home through streets and
    parks

and quiet women, coming to their doors,
then turning away, their struck lives gathered
    around them.

Prayer

Some days, although we cannot pray, a prayer
utters itself. So, a woman will lift
her head from the sieve of her hands and stare
at the minims sung by a tree, a sudden gift.

Some nights, although we are faithless, the truth
enters our hearts, that small familiar pain;
then a man will stand stock-still, hearing his youth
in the distant Latin chanting of a train.

Pray for us now. Grade I piano scales
console the lodger looking out across
a Midlands town. Then dusk, and someone calls
a child's name as though they named their loss.

Darkness outside. Inside, the radio's prayer —
Rockall. Malin. Dogger. Finisterre.

Carol Ann Duffy

Exodus

For all mothers in anguish
Pushing out their babies
In a small basket

To let the river cradle them
And kind hands find
And nurture them

Providing safety
In a hostile world:
Our constant gratitude.

As in this last century
The crowded trains
Taking us away from home

Became our baby baskets
Rattling to foreign parts
Our exodus from death.

Lotte Kramer   61

My children

I can hear them talking, my children
fluent English and broken Kurdish.

And whenever I disagree with them
they will comfort each other by saying:
Don't worry about mum, she's Kurdish.

Will I be the foreigner in my own home?

Choman Hardi

'Let a place be made'

Let a place be made for the one who draws near,
The one who is cold, deprived of any home,

Tempted by the sound of a lamp, by the lit
Threshold of a solitary house.

And if he is still exhausted, full of anguish,
Say again for him those words that heal.

What does this heart which once was silence need
If not those words which are both sign and prayer,

Like a fire caught sight of in the sudden night,
Like the table glimpsed in a poor house?

Yves Bonnefoy
Translated by Anthony Rudolf

Seasons
'An' a so de seasons mix'

Promise

Remember, the time of year
when the future appears
like a blank sheet of paper
a clean calendar, a new chance.
On thick white snow

you vow fresh footprints
then watch them go
with the wind's hearty gust.
Fill your glass. Here's tae us. Promises
made to be broken, made to last.

Jackie Kay

Up in the Morning Early

Cauld blaws the wind frae east to west,
  The drift is driving sairly;
Sae loud and shrill's I hear the blast,
  I'm sure it's winter fairly.

Up in the morning's no for me,
  Up in the morning early;
When a' the hills are cover'd wi' snaw,
  I'm sure it's winter fairly.

The birds sit chittering in the thorn,
  A' day they fare but sparely;
And lang's the night frae e'en to morn,
  I'm sure it's winter fairly.

Up in the morning's no for me,
  Up in the morning early;
When a' the hills are cover'd wi' snaw,
  I'm sure it's winter fairly.

February – not everywhere

Such days, when trees run downwind,
their arms stretched before them.

Such days, when the sun's in a drawer
and the drawer locked.

When the meadow is dead, is a carpet,
thin and shabby, with no pattern

and at bus stops people retract into collars
their faces like fists.

– And when, in a firelit room, a mother looks
at her four seasons, at her little boy,

in the centre of everything, with still pools
of shadows and a fire throwing flowers.

Norman MacCaig

Thaw

The season midnight: glass
cracks with cold. From lighted shop-windows

girls half-sleeping, numb with frost step out.
We warm their hands between our hands, we kiss them

awake, and the planets
melt on their cheeks.

First touch, first tears. Behind their blue eyes darkness
shatters its pane of ice. We

step through into a forest
of sunlight, sunflowers.

Wet Evening in April

The birds sang in the wet trees
And as I listened to them it was a hundred years from now
And I was dead and someone else was listening to them.
But I was glad I had recorded for him
   The melancholy.

Patrick Kavanagh

Seed   The first warm day of spring
and I step out into the garden from the gloom
of a house where hope had died
to tally the storm damage, to seek what may
have survived. And finding some forgotten
lupins I'd sown from seed last autumn
holding in their fingers a raindrop each
like a peace offering, or a promise,
I am suddenly grateful and would
offer a prayer if I believed in God.
But not believing, I bless the power of seed,
its casual, useful persistence,
and bless the power of sun,
its conspiracy with the underground,
and thank my stars the winter's ended.

Proud Songsters

The thrushes sing as the sun is going,
And the finches whistle in ones and pairs,
And as it gets dark loud nightingales
      In bushes
Pipe, as they can when April wears,
    As if all Time were theirs.

These are brand-new birds of twelve-months' growing,
Which a year ago, or less than twain,
No finches were, nor nightingales,
      Nor thrushes,
But only particles of grain,
    And earth, and air, and rain.

Thomas Hardy

Home-Thoughts, from Abroad

Oh, to be in England
Now that April's there,
And whoever wakes in England
Sees, some morning, unaware,
That the lowest boughs and the brushwood
   sheaf
Round the elm-tree bole are in tiny leaf,
While the chaffinch sings on the orchard
   bough
In England – now!

And after April, when May follows,
And the whitethroat builds, and all the swallows!
Hark, where my blossomed pear-tree in the hedge
Leans to the field and scatters on the clover
Blossoms and dewdrops – at the bent spray's edge –
That's the wise thrush; he sings each song twice
   over,
Lest you should think he never could recapture
The first fine careless rapture!
And though the fields look rough with hoary dew,
All will be gay when noontide wakes anew
The buttercups, the little children's dower
– Far brighter than this gaudy melon-flower!

Virtue

Sweet day, so cool, so calm, so bright,
The bridal of the earth and sky:
The dew shall weep thy fall tonight;
                    For thou must die.

Sweet rose, whose hue angry and brave
Bids the rash gazer wipe his eye:
Thy root is ever in its grave,
                    And thou must die.

Sweet spring, full of sweet days and roses,
A box where sweets compacted lie;
My music shows ye have your closes,
                    And all must die.

Only a sweet and virtuous soul,
Like seasoned timber, never gives;
But though the whole world turn to coal,
                    Then chiefly lives.

George Herbert

A Prehistoric Camp

It was the time of year
  Pale lambs leap with thick leggings on
Over small hills that are not there,
  That I climbed Eggardon.

The hedgerows still were bare,
  None ever knew so late a year;
Birds built their nests in the open air,
  Love conquering their fear.

But there on the hill-crest,
  Where only larks or stars look down,
Earthworks exposed a vaster nest,
  Its race of men long flown.

Song: On May Morning

Now the bright morning star, day's harbinger,
Comes dancing from the east, and leads with her
The flowery May, who from her green lap throws
The yellow cowslip, and the pale primrose.
   Hail bounteous May that dost inspire
   Mirth and youth and warm desire!
   Woods and groves are of thy dressing,
   Hill and dale doth boast thy blessing.
Thus we salute thee with our early song,
And welcome thee, and wish thee long.

John Milton

'Now welcome Summer'

Now welcome Summer with thy sunné soft,
That hast this winter's weathers overshake,
And driven away the longé nightés black.

Saint Valentine, that art full high aloft,
Thus singen smallé fowlés for thy sake:
Now welcome Summer with thy sunné soft,
That hast this winter's weathers overshake.

Well have they causé for to gladden oft,
Since each of them recovered hath his make.
Full blissful may they singé when they wake:
Now welcome Summer with thy sunné soft,
That hast this winter's weathers overshake,
And driven away the longé nightés black!

Cut Grass

Cut grass lies frail:
Brief is the breath
Mown stalks exhale.
Long, long the death

It dies in the white hours
Of young-leafed June
With chestnut flowers,
With hedges snowlike strewn,

White lilac bowed,
Lost lanes of Queen Anne's lace,
And that high-builded cloud
Moving at summer's pace.

Philip Larkin

'Sumer is icumen in'

Sumer is icumen in,
Loud sing cuckoo!
Groweth seed and bloweth mead
And springeth the wood now.
Sing cuckoo!

Ewe bleateth after lamb,
Cow loweth after calf,
Bullock starteth, buck farteth,
Merry sing cuckoo!

Cuckoo, cuckoo!
Well singest thou cuckoo,
Nor cease thou never now!

Sing cuckoo now, sing cuckoo!
Sing cuckoo, sing cuckoo now!

Midsummer, Tobago

Broad sun-stoned beaches.

White heat.
A green river.

A bridge,
scorched yellow palms

from the summer-sleeping house
drowsing through August.

Days I have held,
days I have lost,

days that outgrow, like daughters,
my harbouring arms.

Derek Walcott

'Autumn evening'

Autumn evening—
A crow on a bare branch.

Matsuo Bashō
Translated by Kenneth Rexroth

Sonnet 73: 'That time of year thou mayst in me behold'

That time of year thou mayst in me behold
When yellow leaves, or none, or few, do hang
Upon those boughs which shake against the cold,
Bare ruined choirs, where late the sweet birds sang.
In me thou seest the twilight of such day
As after sunset fadeth in the west;
Which by and by black night doth take away,
Death's second self, that seals up all in rest.
In me thou seest the glowing of such fire,
That on the ashes of his youth doth lie,
As the deathbed whereon it must expire,
Consumed with that which it was nourished by.
   This thou perceiv'st, which makes thy love more strong,
   To love that well, which thou must leave ere long.

William Shakespeare

A song for England

An' a so de rain a-fall
An' a so de snow a-rain

An' a so de fog a-fall
An' a so de sun a-fail

An' a so de seasons mix
An' a so de bag-o'-tricks

But a so me understan'
De misery o' de Englishman.

Snow

In the gloom of whiteness,
In the great silence of snow,
A child was sighing
And bitterly saying: 'Oh,
They have killed a white bird up there on her nest,
The down is fluttering from her breast!'
And still it fell through that dusky brightness
On the child crying for the bird of the snow.

Edward Thomas

Winter Travels

who's typing on the void
too many stories
they're twelve stones
hitting the clockface
twelve swans
flying out of winter

tongues in the night
describe gleams of light
blind bells
cry out for someone absent

entering the room
you see that jester's
entered winter
leaving behind flame

Bei Dao
Translated by David Hinton with Yanbing Chen

The Natural World
'Long live the weeds and the wilderness'

For the Life of This Planet

The way the red sun surrenders
its wholeness to curving ocean
bit by bit. The way curving ocean
gives birth to the birth of stars
in the growing darkness,
wearing everything in its path
to cosmic smoothness.
The impulse of stones rolling
towards their own roundness.
The unexpected comets of flying fish.
And Forest, Great-Breathing-Spirit,
rooting to the very end
for the life of this planet.

Grace Nichols

Rainforest

The forest drips and glows with green.
The tree-frog croaks his far-off song.
His voice is stillness, moss and rain
drunk from the forest ages long.

We cannot understand that call
unless we move into his dream,
where all is one and one is all
and frog and python are the same.

We with our quick dividing eyes
measure, distinguish and are gone.
The forest burns, the tree-frog dies,
yet one is all and all are one.

The Tyger

Tyger Tyger, burning bright,
In the forests of the night:
What immortal hand or eye,
Could frame thy fearful symmetry?

In what distant deeps or skies
Burnt the fire of thine eyes!
On what wings dare he aspire?
What the hand, dare sieze the fire?

And what shoulder, & what art,
Could twist the sinews of thy heart?
And when thy heart began to beat,
What dread hand? & what dread feet?

What the hammer? what the chain?
In what furnace was thy brain?
What the anvil? what dread grasp,
Dare its deadly terrors clasp?

When the stars threw down their spears
And water'd heaven with their tears:
Did he smile his work to see?
Did he who made the Lamb make thee?

Tyger Tyger, burning bright,
In the forests of the night:
What immortal hand or eye,
Dare frame thy fearful symmetry?

William Blake

Living

The fire in leaf and grass
so green it seems
each summer the last summer.

The wind blowing, the leaves
shivering in the sun,
each day the last day.

A red salamander
so cold and so
easy to catch, dreamily

moves his delicate feet
and long tail. I hold
my hand open for him to go.

Each minute the last minute.

The Trees

The trees are coming into leaf
Like something almost being said;
The recent buds relax and spread,
Their greenness is a kind of grief.

Is it that they are born again
And we grow old? No, they die too.
Their yearly trick of looking new
Is written down in rings of grain.

Yet still the unresting castles thresh
In fullgrown thickness every May.
Last year is dead, they seem to say,
Begin afresh, afresh, afresh.

Philip Larkin

Everything Changes
after Brecht, 'Alles wandelt sich'

Everything changes. We plant
trees for those born later
but what's happened has happened,
and poisons poured into the seas
cannot be drained out again.

What's happened has happened.
Poisons poured into the seas
cannot be drained out again, but
everything changes. We plant
trees for those born later.

Ragwort

They won't let railways alone, those yellow flowers.
They're that remorseless joy of dereliction
darkest banks exhale like vivid breath
as bricks divide to let them root between.
How every falling place concocts their smile,
taking what's left and making a song of it.

Anne Stevenson

Coltsfoot and Larches

I love coltsfoot that they
Make their appearance into life among dead grass:
Larches, that they
Die colourfully among sombre immortals.

Silver

Slowly, silently, now the moon
Walks the night in her silver shoon;
This way, and that, she peers, and sees
Silver fruit upon silver trees;
One by one the casements catch
Her beams beneath the silvery thatch;
Couched in his kennel, like a log,
With paws of silver sleeps the dog;
From their shadowy cote the white breasts peep
Of doves in a silver-feathered sleep;
A harvest mouse goes scampering by,
With silver claws, and silver eye;
And moveless fish in the water gleam
By silver reeds in a silver stream.

Walter de la Mare

The bee dance

Let the grey dust thicken on the landings,
let the spiders tick in the wall,
let the locks rust and the keys be lost.

This is the yellow hive of my skull
where the bees dance on the honeycomb
their tales of direction and distance.

They tell how high the sun is, how far
to sweet marjoram, borage and thyme,
and the tall green masts of the sunflowers.

The Twa Corbies

As I was walking all alane,
I heard twa corbies making a mane;
The tane unto the tither say,
'Whar sall we gang and dine the day?'

'In behint yon auld fail dyke,
I wot there lies a new-slain knight;
And naebody kens that he lies there,
But his hawk, his hound, and lady fair.

'His hound is to the hunting gane,
His hawk to fetch the wild-fowl hame,
His lady's ta'en another mate,
Sae we may mak our dinner sweet.

'Ye'll sit on his white hause-bane,
And I'll pike out his bonnie blue een:
Wi' ae lock o' his gowden hair
We'll theek our nest when it grows bare.

'Mony a one for him makes mane,
But nane sall ken whar he is gane;
O'er his white banes, when they are bare,
The wind sall blaw for evermair.'

Anon.

Swallows

The swallows are italic again,
cutting their sky-jive
between the telephone wires,
flying in crossed lines.

Their annual regeneration
so flawless to human eyes
that there is no seam
between parent and child.

Just always the swallows
and their script of descenders,
dipping their ink to sign their signatures
across the page of the sky.

Industrial

From a bridge, the inverted *vanitas*
Of a swan drifting down a black canal
Between two corrugated warehouses.

Frances Leviston

An Old Pit Pony

An old pit pony walks
its chalks
across a blasted heath.

Its coat is a cloud hung on a line.

It sighs
for the pit-propped skies
of that world beneath.

Its coat is a cloud hung on a line.

Emmonsails Heath in Winter

I love to see the old heaths withered brake
Mingle its crimpled leaves with furze and ling
While the old heron from the lonely lake
Starts slow and flaps his melancholly wing
And oddling crow in idle motions swing
On the half rotten ash trees topmost twig
Beside whose trunk the gipsey makes his bed
Up flies the bouncing woodcock from the brig
Where a black quagmire quakes beneath the tread
The fieldfare chatters in the whistling thorn
And for the awe round fields and closen rove
And coy bumbarrels twenty in a drove
Flit down the hedgerows in the frozen plain
And hang on little twigs and start again

John Clare

Awe: Haw.　*Closen*: Small enclosed fields.　*Bumbarrels*: Long-tailed tits.

Inversnaid

This darksome burn, horseback brown,
His rollrock highroad roaring down,
In coop and in comb the fleece of his
    foam
Flutes and low to the lake falls home.

A windpuff-bonnet of fawn-froth
Turns and twindles over the broth
Of a pool so pitchblack, fell-frowning,
It rounds and rounds Despair to
    drowning.

Degged with dew, dappled with dew
Are the groins of the braes that the brook treads
    through,
Wiry heathpacks, flitches of fern,
And the beadbonny ash that sits over the burn.

What would the world be, once bereft
Of wet and of wildness? Let them be left,
O let them be left, wildness and wet;
Long live the weeds and the wilderness yet.

Families
'I am the family face'

Heredity

I am the family face;
Flesh perishes, I live on,
Projecting trait and trace
Through time to times anon,
And leaping from place to place
Over oblivion.

The years-heired feature that can
In curve and voice and eye
Despise the human span
Of durance – that is I;
The eternal thing in man,
That heeds no call to die.

Thomas Hardy

New Gravity

Treading through the half-light of ivy
and headstone, I see you in the distance
as I'm telling our daughter
about this place, this whole business:
a sister about to be born,
how a life's new gravity suspends in water.
Under the oak, the fallen leaves
are pieces of the tree's jigsaw;
by your father's grave you are pressing acorns
into the shadows to seed.

Child Your clear eye is the one absolutely beautiful thing.
I want to fill it with colour and ducks,
The zoo of the new

Whose names you meditate—
April snowdrop, Indian pipe,
Little

Stalk without wrinkle,
Pool in which images
Should be grand and classical

Not this troublous
Wringing of hands, this dark
Ceiling without a star.

Sylvia Plath

Full Moon and Little Frieda

A cool small evening shrunk to a dog bark and
   the clank of a bucket –

And you listening.
A spider's web, tense for the dew's touch.
A pail lifted, still and brimming – mirror
To tempt a first star to a tremor.

Cows are going home in the lane there, looping
   the hedges with their warm wreaths of breath –
A dark river of blood, many boulders,
Balancing unspilled milk.

'Moon!' you cry suddenly, 'Moon! Moon!'

The moon has stepped back like an artist
   gazing amazed at a work
That points at him amazed.

To My Daughter

Bright clasp of her whole hand around my finger
My daughter, as we walk together now.
All my life I'll feel a ring invisibly
Circle this bone with shining: when she is grown
Far from today as her eyes are far already.

Stephen Spender

Spacetime

When I grow up and you get small,
then—

(In Kaluza's theory the fifth dimension
is represented as a circle
associated with every point
in spacetime)

— then when I die, I'll never be alive again?
Never.
Never never?
Never never.
Yes, but never never never?
No . . . not never never never,
just never never.

So we made
a small family contribution
to the quantum problem of eleven-dimensional supergravity.

Miroslav Holub
Translated by David Young and Dana Hábová

To My Dear and Loving Husband

If ever two were one, then surely we.
If ever man were loved by wife, then thee;
If ever wife was happy in a man,
Compare with me ye women if you can.
I prize thy love more than whole mines of gold,
Or all the riches that the East doth hold.
My love is such that rivers cannot quench,
Nor aught but love from thee give recompence.
Thy love is such I can no way repay,
The heavens reward thee manifold I pray.
Then while we live, in love let's so persever,
That when we live no more, we may live ever.

Anne Bradstreet

Should You Die First

Let me at least collect your smells
as specimens: your armpits, woollen sweater,
fingers yellow from smoke. I'd need
to take an imprint of your foot
and make recordings of your laugh.

These archives I shall carry into exile;
my body a St Helena where ships no longer dock,
a rock in the ocean, an outpost where the wind howls
and polar bears beat down the door.

I Am Becoming My Mother

Yellow/brown woman
fingers smelling always of onions

My mother raises rare blooms
and waters them with tea
her birth waters sang like rivers
my mother is now me

My mother had a linen dress
the colour of the sky
and stored lace and damask
tablecloths
to pull shame out of her eye.

I am becoming my mother
brown/yellow woman
fingers smelling always of onions.

Lorna Goodison

Handbag

My mother's old leather handbag,
crowded with letters she carried
all through the war. The smell
of my mother's handbag: mints
and lipstick and Coty powder.
The look of those letters, softened
and worn at the edges, opened,
read, and refolded so often.
Letters from my father. Odour
of leather and powder, which ever
since then has meant womanliness,
and love, and anguish, and war.

Memory of my Father

Every old man I see
Reminds me of my father
When he had fallen in love with death
One time when sheaves were gathered.

That man I saw in Gardner Street
Stumble on the kerb was one,
He stared at me half-eyed,
I might have been his son.

And I remember the musician
Faltering over his fiddle
In Bayswater, London,
He too set me the riddle.

Every old man I see
In October-coloured weather
Seems to say to me:
'I was once your father.'

Patrick Kavanagh

Taid's Grave

Rain on lilac leaves. In the dusk
they show me the grave,
a casket of stars underfoot,
his name there, and his language.

Voice of thrushes in rain.
My cousin Gwynfor eases me
into the green cave.
Wet hands of lilac

touch my wrist and the secret
unfreckled underside of my arm
daring fingers to count
five warm blue eggs.

Taid: Grandfather.

Out There

'We live in a world of motion and distance'

Distances

(After Jaccottet)

Swifts turn in the heights of the air;
higher still turn the invisible stars.
When day withdraws to the ends of the earth
their fires shine on a dark expanse of sand.

We live in a world of motion and distance.
The heart flies from tree to bird,
from bird to distant star,
from star to love; and love grows
in the quiet house, turning and working,
servant of thought, a lamp held in one hand.

Derek Mahon

Delay

The radiance of that star that leans on me
Was shining years ago. The light that now
Glitters up there my eye may never see,
And so the time lag teases me with how

Love that loves now may not reach me until
Its first desire is spent. The star's impulse
Must wait for eyes to claim it beautiful
And love arrived may find us somewhere else.

The Present

For the present there is just one moon,
though every level pond gives back
   another.

But the bright disc shining in the black
   lagoon,
perceived by astrophysicist and lover,

is milliseconds old. And even that light's
seven minutes older than its source.

And the stars we think we see on
   moonless nights
are long extinguished. And, of course,

this very moment, as you read this line,
is literally gone before you know it.

Forget the here-and-now. We have no time
but this device of wantonness and wit.

Make me this present then: your hand in mine,
and we'll live out our lives in it.

Michael Donaghy

Out There

If space begins at an indefinite zone
where the chance of two gas molecules
    colliding
is rarer than a green dog or a blue moon
then that's as near as we can get to nothing.

Nostalgia for the earth and its atmosphere
weakens the flesh and bones of cosmonauts.
One woke to find his crewmate in a space suit
and asked where he was going. For a walk.

He had to sleep between him and the air-lock.
Another heard a dog bark and a child cry
halfway to the moon. What once had been

where heaven was, is barren beyond imagining,
and never so keenly as from out there can
the lost feel earth's the only paradise.

It looks so simple from a distance...

The way lives touch,
touch and spring apart,
the pulse synaptic,
local, but its stretch
electric — as when cities
lose themselves in velvet
under winking planes,
binding black hostilities
with gold chains.

Anne Stevenson

Stars and planets

Trees are cages for them: water holds its breath
To balance them without smudging on its delicate meniscus.
Children watch them playing in their heavenly playground;
Men use them to lug ships across oceans, through firths.

They seem so twinkle-still, but they never cease
Inventing new spaces and huge explosions
And migrating in mathematical tribes over
The steppes of space at their outrageous ease.

It's hard to think that the earth is one—
This poor sad bearer of wars and disasters
Rolls-Roycing round the sun with its load of gangsters,
Attended only by the loveless moon.

On Lake Nicaragua

Slow cargo-launch, midnight, mid-lake,
bound from San Miguelito to Granada.
The lights ahead not yet in sight,
the dwindling ones behind completely gone.
Only the stars
(the mast a finger pointing to the Seven Sisters)
                    and the moon, rising above Chontales.

Another launch (just one red light) goes by
and sinks into the night.
We, for them:

                  another red light sinking in the night . . .
And I, watching the stars, lying on the deck
between bunches of bananas and Chontales cheeses,
wonder: perhaps there's one that is an earth like ours
and someone's watching me (watching the stars)
from another launch, on another night, on another lake.

Ernesto Cardenal
Translated by Ernesto Cardenal and Robert Pring-Mill

Benediction

Thanks to the ear
that someone may hear

Thanks to seeing
that someone may see

Thanks to feeling
that someone may feel

Thanks to touch
that one may be touched

Thanks to flowering of white moon
and spreading shawl of black night
holding villages and cities together

James Berry

Canticle

Sometimes when you walk down to the red gate
hearing the scrape-music of your shoes across gravel,
a yellow moon will lift over the hill;
you swing the gate shut and lean on the topmost bar
as if something has been accomplished in the world;
a night wind mistles through the poplar leaves
and all the noise of the universe stills
to an oboe hum, the given note of a perfect
music; there is a vast sky wholly dedicated
to the stars and you know, with certainty,
that all the dead are out, up there, in one
holiday flotilla, and that they celebrate
the fact of a red gate and a yellow moon
that tunes their instruments with you to the symphony.

Road

Traveller, your footprints are
the only path, the only track:
wayfarer, there is no way,
there is no map or Northern star,
just a blank page and a starless dark;
and should you turn round to admire
the distance that you've made today
the road will billow into dust.
No way on and no way back,
there is no way, my comrade: trust
your own quick step, the end's delay,
the vanished trail of your own wake,
wayfarer, sea-walker, Christ.

Don Paterson

The River Road

Come for a walk down the river road,
For though you're all a long time dead
The waters part to let us pass

The way we'd go on summer nights
In the times we were children
And thought we were lovers.

The river road led to the end of it all –
Stones and pale water, the lightship's bell
And distance we never looked into.

A long time gone
And the river road with it.
No margin to keep us in mind.

For afterlife, only beginning, beginning,
Wide, dark waters that grow in the telling,
Where the river road carries us now.

The Way We Go

the way we go about our lives
trying out each empty room
like houses we might own
eavesdropping for clues in corridors until

standing at a gate or attic window
seeing beauty in a flag of sky
we're gone, leaving the doors open
all the lights burning

Katharine Towers

'Thread suns'

Thread suns
above the grey-black wilderness.
A tree-
high thought
tunes in to light's pitch: there are
still songs to be sung on the other side
of mankind.

Paul Celan
Translated by Michael Hamburger

'I saw a man pursuing the horizon'

I saw a man pursuing the horizon;
Round and round they sped.
I was disturbed at this;
I accosted the man.
'It is futile,' I said,
'You can never –'

'You lie,' he cried,
And ran on.

Stephen Crane

Song in Space

When man first flew beyond the sky
He looked back into the world's blue eye.

Man said: What makes your eye so blue?
Earth said: The tears in the oceans do.

Why are the seas so full of tears?
Because I've wept so many thousand years.

Why do you weep as you dance through space?
Because I am the mother of the human race.

Dreams

'I, being poor, have only my dreams'

Dreams

Here we are all, by day; by night we're hurled
By dreams, each one, into a several world.

Robert Herrick

Disillusionment of Ten O'Clock

The houses are haunted
By white night-gowns.
None are green,
Or purple with green rings,
Or green with yellow rings,
Or yellow with blue rings.
None of them are strange,
With socks of lace
And beaded ceintures.
People are not going
To dream of baboons and periwinkles.
Only, here and there, an old sailor,
Drunk and asleep in his boots,
Catches tigers
In red weather.

He wishes for the Cloths of Heaven

Had I the heavens' embroidered cloths,
Enwrought with golden and silver light,
The blue and the dim and the dark cloths
Of night and light and the half-light,
I would spread the cloths under your feet:
But I, being poor, have only my dreams;
I have spread my dreams under your feet;
Tread softly because you tread on my dreams.

W. B. Yeats

The Reassurance

About ten days or so
After we saw you dead
You came back in a dream.
I'm all right now you said.

And it *was* you, although
You were fleshed out again:
You hugged us all round then,
And gave your welcoming beam.

How like you to be kind,
Seeking to reassure.
And, yes, how like my mind
To make itself secure.

Dream

I am become a stranger to my dreams,
Their places unknown. A bridge there was
Over the lovely waters of the Tyne, my mother
Was with me, we were almost there,
It seemed, but in that almost opened up a valley
Extending and expanding, wind-sculptured sand;
Dry its paths, a beautiful waterless waste
Without one green leaf, sand-coloured behind closed eyes.
That film shifts, but the arid place remains
When day returns. Yet we were still going towards the Tyne,
That green river-side where childhood's flowers
Were growing still, my mother and I, she dead,
With me for ever in that dream.

Kathleen Raine

Waiting for Rain in Devon

Rain here on a tableau of cows
might seem a return to everyday—
why, you can almost poach
the trout with your hands,
their element has so thickened!
Something has emerged from dreams
to show us where we are going,
a journey to a desolate star.
Come back, perennial rain,
stand your soft sculptures in our gardens
for the barefoot frogs to leap.

Rain Travel

I wake in the dark and remember
it is the morning when I must start
by myself on the journey
I lie listening to the black hour
before dawn and you are
still asleep beside me while
around us the trees full of night lean
hushed in their dream that bears
us up asleep and awake then I hear
drops falling one by one into
the sightless leaves and I
do not know when they began but
all at once there is no sound but rain
and the stream below us roaring
away into the rushing darkness

W. S. Merwin

The Creel

The world began with a woman,
shawl-happed, stooped under a creel,
whose slow step you recognize
from troubled dreams. You feel

obliged to help bear her burden
from hill or kelp-strewn shore,
but she passes by unseeing
thirled to her private chore.

It's not sea birds or peat she's carrying,
not fleece, nor the herring bright
but her fear that if ever she put it down
the world would go out like a light.

Creel: Wicker basket for carrying fish, peat, etc. on the back.   *Thirled*: Enslaved.

Freight song

We were lying, the two of us
on a freight lift platform

which four angels were hoisting up,
their haloes journeying

little by little up to blue sky.
And you were stacked next to me

and I was stacked alongside you
like two symbiotic suitcases

with labels reading: The Twilit Sky.
Our sleepy lift attendants

were the stars of heaven.
And we were the goods —

Judith Kazantzis

Tortoise

Under the mottled shell of the old tortoise
beats the heart of a young dancer.

She dreams of twirling on table-tops,
turning cartwheels,
kicking up her heels at the Carnival ball.

'Oh, who will kiss my cold and wrinkled lips,
and set my dreaming spirit free?'

The Two Apes of Brueghel

Here's my dream of a final exam:
two apes, in chains, sitting at a window.
Outside the sky is flying
and the sea bathes.

I am taking the test on human history.
I stammer and blunder.

One ape, staring at me, listens with irony,
the other seems to doze –
but when I am silent after a question,
she prompts me
with a soft clanking of the chain.

Wisława Szymborska
Translated by Grazyna Drabik with Sharon Olds

Viv
for cricketer, Vivian Richards

Like the sun rising and setting
Like the thunderous roar of a bull rhino
Like the sleek, quick grace of a gazelle,
The player springs into the eye
And lights the world with fires
Of a million dreams, a million aspirations.
The batsman-hero climbs the skies,
Strikes the earth-ball for six
And the landscape rolls with the ecstasy of the
    magic play.

Through the covers, the warrior thrusts a majestic cut
Lighting the day with runs
As bodies reel and tumble,
Hands clap, eyes water
And hearts move inside out.

The volcano erupts!
And blows the game apart.

Faustin Charles   149

from Frost at Midnight

The Frost performs its secret ministry
Unhelped by any wind. The owlet's cry
Came loud – and hark, again! loud as before.
The inmates of my cottage, all at rest,
Have left me to that solitude, which suits
Abstruser musings: save that at my side
My cradled infant slumbers peacefully.
'Tis calm indeed! so calm, that it disturbs
And vexes meditation with its strange
And extreme silentness. Sea, hill, and wood,
This populous village! Sea, and hill, and wood,
With all the numberless goings-on of life,
Inaudible as dreams!

Samuel Taylor Coleridge

The Rescue

In drifts of sleep I came upon you
Buried to your waist in snow.
You reached your arms out: I came to
Like water in a dream of thaw.

Music
'The insidious mastery of song'

'Music, when soft voices die'
To [Emilia Viviani]

Music, when soft voices die,
Vibrates in the memory—
Odours, when sweet violets sicken,
Live within the sense they quicken.

Rose leaves, when the rose is dead,
Are heaped for the beloved's bed—
And so thy thoughts, when thou art gone,
Love itself shall slumber on . . .

Percy Bysshe Shelley

Piano

Softly, in the dusk, a woman is singing to me;
Taking me back down the vista of years, till I see
A child sitting under the piano, in the boom of the tingling strings
And pressing the small, poised feet of a mother who smiles as she sings.

In spite of myself, the insidious mastery of song
Betrays me back, till the heart of me weeps to belong
To the old Sunday evenings at home, with winter outside
And hymns in the cosy parlour, the tinkling piano our guide.

So now it is vain for the singer to burst into clamour
With the great black piano appassionato. The glamour
Of childish days is upon me, my manhood is cast
Down in the flood of remembrance, I weep like a child for the past.

Naima

for John Coltrane

Propped against the crowded bar
he pours into the curved and silver horn
his old unhappy longing for a home

the dancers twist and turn
he leans and wishes he could burn
his memories to ashes like some old notorious emperor

of rome. but no stars blazed across the sky when he was born
no wise men found his hovel. this crowded bar
where dancers twist and turn

holds all the fame and recognition he will ever earn
on earth or heaven. he leans against the bar
and pours his old unhappy longing in the saxophone

Kamau Brathwaite

'The silver swan'

The silver swan, who living had no note,
When death approached unlocked her silent throat,
Leaning her breast against the reedy shore,
Thus sung her first and last, and sung no more:
Farewell all joys, O death come close mine eyes,
More geese than swans now live, more fools than wise.

Concerto for Double Bass

He is a drunk leaning companionably
Around a lamp post or doing up
With intermittent concentration
Another drunk's coat.

He is a polite but devoted Valentino,
Cheek to cheek, forgetting the next step.
He is feeling the pulse of the fat lady
Or cutting her in half.

But close your eyes and it is sunset
At the edge of the world. It is the language
Of dolphins, the growth of tree-roots,
The heart-beat slowing down.

John Fuller

If Bach Had Been a Beekeeper

for Arvo Pärt

If Bach had been a beekeeper
he would have heard
all those notes
suspended above one another
in the air of his ear
as the differentiated swarm returning
to the exact hive
and place in the hive,
topping up the cells
with the honey of C major,

food for the listening generations,
key to their comfort
and solace of their distress
as they return and return
to those counterpointed levels
of hovering wings where
movement is dance
and the air itself
a scented garden

At Sixty

Dat line whaar birds, hurless, cross
a treshel-tree, winter at der back,
or a skirl o simmer afore dem.

Whaar, alang da sixtieth parallel,
sheerlin on ringin strings vimmers
on a nordern palette. Hingin in

ta tree score year is harkin for dat line,
anidder saison o sang. Hit's pushin
fornenst da door, liftin da sneck, takkin

da fiddle doon an tunin whit's left ta mak
da notes. Fingers rekk farder, trivvel
da missin string, tize oot da melody.

Christine De Luca

Hurless: Exhausted. *Treshel-tree*: Threshold. *Skirl*: Shrill laugh. *Sheerlin*: Singing (of birds). *Ringin strings*: Resonance when playing the fiddle.
Vimmers: Trembles. *Tree*: Three. *Fornenst*: Against. *Sneck*: Latch. *Rekk*: Reach. *Farder*: Further. *Trivvel*: Grope gently. *Tize*: Tempt, entice.

Cradle Song

Golden slumbers kiss your eyes,
Smiles awake you when you rise;
Sleep, pretty wantons, do not cry,
And I will sing a lullaby,
Rock them, rock them, lullaby.

Care is heavy, therefore sleep you,
You are care, and care must keep you;
Sleep, pretty wantons, do not cry,
And I will sing a lullaby,
Rock them, rock them, lullaby.

Ariel's Song: 'Full fathom five'

Full fathom five thy father lies,
  Of his bones are coral made;
Those are pearls that were his eyes,
  Nothing of him that doth fade,
But doth suffer a sea-change
Into something rich and strange.
Sea-nymphs hourly ring his knell—
  Hark! now I hear them,
     Ding-dong bell.

William Shakespeare

Song from Comus: 'Sabrina fair'

Attendant Spirit: Sabrina fair,
   Listen where thou art sitting
Under the glassy, cool, translucent wave,
   In twisted braids of lilies knitting
The loose train of thy amber-dropping hair;
   Listen for dear honour's sake,
   Goddess of the silver lake,
     Listen and save.

Sabrina: By the rushy-fringèd bank,
Where grows the willow and the osier dank,
   My sliding chariot stays,
Thick set with agate, and the azurn sheen
Of turquoise blue, and emerald green,
   That in the channel strays;
Whilst from off the waters fleet
Thus I set my printless feet
O'er the cowslip's velvet head,
   That bends not as I tread.
Gentle swain at thy request
    I am here.

John Milton   163

Maire Macrae's Song

The singer is old and has forgotten
Her girlhood's grief for the young soldier
Who sailed away across the ocean,
Love's brief joy and lonely sorrow:
The song is older than the singer.

The song is older than the singer
Shaped by the love and the long waiting
Of women dead and long forgotten
Who sang before remembered time
To teach the unbroken heart its sorrow.

The girl who waits for her young soldier
Learns from the cadence of a song
How deep her love, how long the waiting.
Sorrow is older than the heart,
Already old when love is young:
The song is older than the sorrow.

Kathleen Raine

A Tune

A foolish rhythm turns in my idle head
As a wind-mill turns in the wind on an empty sky.
Why is it when love, which men call deathless, is dead,
That memory, men call fugitive, will not die?
Is love not dead? Yet I hear that tune if I lie
Dreaming awake in the night on my lonely bed,
And an old thought turns with the old tune in my head
As a wind-mill turns in the wind on an empty sky.

Sense and Nonsense
'Grof grawff gahf?'

Nasturtium Scanned

Ropey, lippy, loopy, scribbly
over a brick's edge,
she's a riot,
straggly as random and tricky as a diet,
tiddly, wobbly, oddly nibbly
and flashy as a landmine on her vine-meandrine
Alexandrine tangle-scanned line.

Judith Rodriguez

The Loch Ness Monster's Song

Sssnnnwhufffffll?
Hnwhuffl hhnnwfl hnfl hfl?
Gdroblboblhobngbl gbl gl g g g g glbgl.
Drublhaflablhaflubhafgabhaflhafl fl fl—
gm grawwwww grf grawf awfgm graw gm.
Hovoplodok-doplodovok-plovodokot-doplodokosh?
Splgraw fok fok splgrafhatchgabrlgabrl fok splfok!
Zgra kra gka fok!
Grof grawff gahf?
Gombl mbl bl—
blm plm,
blm plm,
blm plm,
blp.

'I saw a Peacock with a fiery tail'

I saw a Peacock with a fiery tail
I saw a blazing Comet drop down hail
I saw a Cloud with Ivy circled round
I saw a sturdy Oak creep on the ground
I saw a Pismire swallow up a Whale
I saw a raging Sea brim full of Ale
I saw a Venice Glass sixteen foot deep
I saw a Well full of men's tears that weep
I saw their Eyes all in a flame of fire
I saw a House as big as the Moon and higher
I saw the Sun even in the midst of night
I saw the Man that saw this wondrous sight.

Anon.

The Leader

I wanna be the leader
I wanna be the leader
Can I be the leader?
Can I? I can?
Promise? Promise?
Yippee, I'm the leader
I'm the leader

OK what shall we do?

Into Rail

The first train I rode in I rode in when I was eight
it was a beautiful beast, a great
one-nostrilled, black dragon
cheerfully dragging its human wagon loads.
Now the nostrils have gone
but the benevolence goes on.
The loco lives
the loco gives.
Even the trains
I do not catch
transport me.

John Hegley

Sun a-shine, rain a-fall

Sun a-shine an' rain a-fall,
The Devil an' him wife cyan 'gree at all,
The two o' them want one fish-head,
The Devil call him wife bonehead,
She hiss her teeth, call him cock-eye,
Greedy, worthless an' workshy,
While them busy callin' name,
The puss walk in, sey is a shame
To see a nice fish go to was'e,
Lef' with a big grin pon him face.

'There was an Old Man with a beard'

There was an Old Man with a beard,
Who said, 'It is just as I feared! –
    Two Owls and a Hen,
    Four Larks and a Wren,
Have all built their nests in my beard!'

Edward Lear

'I have a gentil cock'

I have a gentil cock
croweth me day
he doth me risen early
my matins for to say

I have a gentil cock
comen he is of great
his comb is of red coral
his tail is of jet

I have a gentil cock
comen he is of kind
his comb is of red sorrel
his tail is of inde

his legs be of azure
so gentil and so small
his spurs are of silver white
into the wortewale

his eyes are of crystal
locked all in amber
and every night he percheth him
in my lady's chamber

Inde: Indigo.   *Wortewale*: The root of the spur.

Anglo-Saxon Riddle

from The Exeter Book

I'm a strange creature, for I satisfy women,
a service to the neighbours! No one suffers
at my hands except for my slayer.
I grow very tall, erect in a bed,
I'm hairy underneath. From time to time
a good-looking girl, the doughty daughter
of some churl dares to hold me,
grips my russet skin, robs me of my head
and puts me in the pantry. At once that girl
with plaited hair who has confined me
remembers our meeting. Her eye moistens.

Anon.
Translated by Kevin Crossley-Holland

Riddle

I was the cause of great troubles,
yet, resting among leaves, I did nothing wrong.
After much waiting I was taken in hand,
passed from one to another.
Broken I moved beyond sharp barriers
and was cradled in wetness, mashed to pulp.
Soon I entered a dark tunnel
where bathed in acids I altered my being.

But what I entered I also altered,
bringing light where there had been darkness.
I brought strife where there had been peace,
pain where there had been comfort.
My journey ended in the place of corruption
but by then I had changed the world.

This Is Just to Say

I have eaten
the plums
that were in
the icebox

and which
you were probably
saving
for breakfast

Forgive me
they were delicious
so sweet
and so cold

William Carlos Williams

giovanni caboto/john cabot

fourteen hundred and ninety seven
giovanni sailed from the coast of devon

  52 days   discovered cape breton n.s.
caught some cod   went home
with 10 bear hides
 (none prime)

told henry 7
his majesty now owned
cipango   land of jewels
abounding moreover in silks
& brasilwode
also the spice islands of asia
& the country of the grand khan

  henry gave giovanni 30 quid
to go back to nova scotia

who was kidding who?

Quark

'Transcendental,' said the technician,
'to stumble on a quark that talks back.
I will become a mystagogue, initiate
punters into the wonder of it for cash.'
'Bollocks,' said the quark, from its aluminium
nacelle. 'I don't need no dodgy
crypto-human strategising my future.
Gonna down-size under the cocoplum
or champak, drink blue marimbas into
the sunset, and play with speaking quarklike
while I beflower the passing gravitons.'

Jo Shapcott

The Uncertainty of the Poet

I am a poet.
I am very fond of bananas.

I am bananas.
I am very fond of a poet.

I am a poet of bananas.
I am very fond.

A fond poet of 'I am, I am' –
Very bananas.

Fond of 'Am I bananas?
Am I?' – a very poet.

Bananas of a poet!
Am I fond? Am I very?

Poet bananas! I am.
I am fond of a 'very '.

I am of very fond bananas.
Am I a poet?

The Lobster Quadrille

'Will you walk a little faster?' said a whiting to a snail,
'There's a porpoise close behind us, and he's treading on my tail.
See how eagerly the lobsters and the turtles all advance!
They are waiting on the shingle – will you come and join the dance?
    Will you, won't you, will you, won't you,
        will you join the dance?
    Will you, won't you, will you, won't you,
        won't you join the dance?

'You can really have no notion how delightful it will be
When they take us up and throw us, with the lobsters, out to sea!'
But the snail replied 'Too far, too far!', and gave a look askance—
Said he thanked the whiting kindly, but he would not join the dance.
   Would not, could not, would not, could not,
      would not join the dance.
   Would not, could not, would not, could not,
      could not join the dance.

                    'What matters it how far we go?' his scaly friend replied,
                    'There is another shore, you know, upon the other side.
                    The further off from England the nearer is to France—
                    Then turn not pale, beloved snail, but come and join
                       the dance.
                       Will you, won't you, will you, won't you,
                          will you join the dance?
                       Will you, won't you, will you, won't you,
                          won't you join the dance?'

The Darker Side
'I have been one acquainted with the night'

Acquainted with the Night

I have been one acquainted with the night.
I have walked out in rain – and back in rain.
I have outwalked the furthest city light.

I have looked down the saddest city lane.
I have passed by the watchman on his beat
And dropped my eyes, unwilling to explain.

I have stood still and stopped the sound of feet
When far away an interrupted cry
Came over houses from another street,

But not to call me back or say good-by;
And further still at an unearthly height
One luminary clock against the sky

Proclaimed the time was neither wrong nor right.
I have been one acquainted with the night.

Robert Frost

'I stepped from Plank to Plank'

I stepped from Plank to Plank
A slow and cautious way
The Stars about my Head I felt
About my Feet the Sea.

I knew not but the next
Would be my final inch—
This gave me that precarious Gait
Some call Experience.

I Am

I am – yet what I am none cares or knows,
My friends forsake me like a memory lost;
I am the self-consumer of my woes,
They rise and vanish in oblivious host
Like shades in love and death's oblivion lost,
And yet I am – and live, with shadows tossed

Into the nothingness of scorn and noise,
Into the living sea of waking dreams,
Where there is neither sense of life nor joys,
But the vast shipwreck of my life's esteems;
And e'en the dearest, that I loved the best,
Are strange – nay, rather stranger than the rest.

I long for scenes where man has never trod,
A place where woman never smiled or wept,
There to abide with my creator, God,
And sleep as I in childhood sweetly slept,
Untroubling and untroubled where I lie;
The grass below – above the vaulted sky.

John Clare

A Glass of Water

Here is a glass of water from my well.
It tastes of rock and root and earth and rain;
It is the best I have, my only spell,
And it is cold, and better than champagne.
Perhaps someone will pass this house one day
To drink, and be restored, and go his way,
Someone in dark confusion as I was
When I drank down cold water in a glass,
Drank a transparent health to keep me sane,
After the bitter mood had gone again.

Sonnet: On His Blindness

When I consider how my light is spent,
    Ere half my days, in this dark world and wide,
    And that one talent which is death to hide,
    Lodged with me useless, though my soul more bent
To serve therewith my Maker, and present
    My true account, lest he returning chide,
    Doth God exact day-labour, light denied,
    I fondly ask; but Patience to prevent
That murmur, soon replies, God doth not need
    Either man's work or his own gifts, who best
    Bear his mild yoke, they serve him best, his state
Is kingly. Thousands at his bidding speed
    And post o'er land and ocean without rest:
    They also serve who only stand and wait.

John Milton

On Himself

Abstracted by silence from the age of seven,
Deafened and penned by as black calamity
As twice to be born, I cannot without pity
Contemplate myself as an infant;

Or fail to speak of silence as a priestess
Calling to serve in the temple of a skull
Her innocent choice. It is barely possible
Not to be affected by such a distress.

They Are Not Long

Vitae summa brevis spem nos vetat incohare longam[*]

They are not long, the weeping and the laughter,
Love and desire and hate:
I think they have no portion in us after
We pass the gate.

They are not long, the days of wine and roses:
Out of a misty dream
Our path emerges for a while, then closes
Within a dream.

Ernest Dowson

[*] 'Life's short span prevents us from entertaining far-off hopes' (Horace).

A 14-Year-Old Convalescent Cat in the Winter

I want him to have another living summer,
to lie in the sun and enjoy the *douceur de vivre*—
because the sun, like golden rum in a rummer,
is what makes an idle cat *un tout petit peu ivre*—

I want him to lie stretched out, contented,
revelling in the heat, his fur all dry and warm,
an Old Age Pensioner, retired, resented
by no one, and happinesses in a beelike swarm

to settle on him — postponed for another season
that last fated hateful journey to the vet
from which there is no return (and age the reason),
which must soon come — as I cannot forget.

When I Have Fears That I May Cease To Be

When I have fears that I may cease to be
  Before my pen has glean'd my teeming brain,
Before high-pilèd books, in charact'ry,
  Hold like rich garners the full-ripen'd grain;
When I behold, upon the night's starr'd face,
  Huge cloudy symbols of a high romance,
And think that I may never live to trace
  Their shadows, with the magic hand of chance;
And when I feel, fair creature of an hour!
  That I shall never look upon thee more,
Never have relish in the faery power
  Of unreflecting love! – then on the shore
Of the wide world I stand alone, and think
Till love and fame to nothingness do sink.

John Keats

Song: 'Fear no more the heat o' the sun'

Fear no more the heat o' the sun,
 Nor the furious winter's rages;
Thou thy worldly task hast done,
 Home art gone, and ta'en thy wages.
Golden lads and girls all must,
As chimney-sweepers, come to dust.

Fear no more the frown o' the great;
 Thou art past the tyrant's stroke;
Care no more to clothe and eat;
 To thee the reed is as the oak.
The sceptre, learning, physic, must
All follow this, and come to dust.

Fear no more the lightning flash,
 Nor th' all-dreaded thunder stone;
Fear not slander, censure rash;
 Thou hast finished joy and moan.
All lovers young, all lovers must
Consign to thee, and come to dust.

Do Not Go Gentle into That Good Night

Do not go gentle into that good night,
Old age should burn and rave at close of day;
Rage, rage against the dying of the light.

Though wise men at their end know dark is right,
Because their words had forked no lightning they
Do not go gentle into that good night.

Good men, the last wave by, crying how
  bright
Their frail deeds might have danced in a
  green bay,
Rage, rage against the dying of the light.

Wild men who caught and sang the sun in
  flight,
And learn, too late, they grieved it on its way,
Do not go gentle into that good night.

Grave men, near death, who see with blinding sight
Blind eyes could blaze like meteors and be gay,
Rage, rage against the dying of the light.

And you, my father, there on the sad height,
Curse, bless, me now with your fierce tears, I pray.
Do not go gentle into that good night.
Rage, rage against the dying of the light.

Coda

Maybe we knew each other better
When the night was young and unrepeated
And the moon stood still over Jericho.

So much for the past; in the present
There are moments caught between heart-beats
When maybe we know each other better.

But what is that clinking in the darkness?
Maybe we shall know each other better
When the tunnels meet beneath the mountain.

Louis MacNeice

Holy Sonnet: 'Death be not proud'

Death be not proud, though some have called thee
Mighty and dreadful, for thou art not so;
For those whom thou think'st thou dost overthrow
Die not, poor Death, nor yet canst thou kill me.
From rest and sleep, which but thy pictures be,
Much pleasure, then from thee much more must flow;
And soonest our best men with thee do go,
Rest of their bones, and soul's delivery.
Thou art slave to fate, chance, kings, and desperate men,
And dost with poison, war, and sickness dwell,
And poppy or charms can make us sleep as well
And better than thy stroke; why swell'st thou then?
One short sleep past, we wake eternally,
And death shall be no more; Death, thou shalt die.

War

'What passing-bells for these
who die as cattle?'

Wind

This is the wind, the wind in a field of corn.
Great crowds are fleeing from a major disaster
Down the long valleys, the green swaying wadis,
Down through the beautiful catastrophe of wind.

Families, tribes, nations and their livestock
Have heard something, seen something. An expectation
Or a gigantic misunderstanding has swept over the hilltop
Bending the ear of the hedgerow with stories of fire and sword.

I saw a thousand years pass in two seconds.
Land was lost, languages rose and divided.
This lord went east and found safety.
His brother sought Africa and a dish of aloes.

Centuries, minutes later, one might ask
How the hilt of a sword wandered so far from the smithy.
And somewhere they will sing: 'Like chaff we were borne
In the wind.' This is the wind in a field of corn.

Map of the New World:
Archipelagoes

At the end of this sentence, rain will begin.
At the rain's edge, a sail.

Slowly the sail will lose sight of islands;
into a mist will go the belief in harbours
of an entire race.

The ten-years war is finished.
Helen's hair, a grey cloud.
Troy, a white ashpit
by the drizzling sea.

The drizzle tightens like the strings of a harp.
A man with clouded eyes picks up the rain
and plucks the first line of the *Odyssey*.

Derek Walcott

Swineherd

When all this is over, said the swineherd,
I mean to retire, where
Nobody will have heard about my special skills
And conversation is mainly about the weather.

I intend to learn how to make coffee, at least as well
As the Portuguese lay-sister in the kitchen
And polish the brass fenders every day.
I want to lie awake at night
Listening to cream crawling to the top of the jug
And the water lying soft in the cistern.

I want to see an orchard where the trees grow in straight lines
And the yellow fox finds shelter between the navy-blue trunks,
Where it gets dark early in summer
And the apple-blossom is allowed to wither on the bough.

Eiléan Ní Chuilleanáin

In Time of 'The Breaking of Nations'*

Only a man harrowing clods
   In a slow silent walk
With an old horse that stumbles and nods
   Half asleep as they stalk.

Only thin smoke without flame
   From the heaps of couch-grass;
Yet this will go onward the same
   Though Dynasties pass.

Yonder a maid and her wight
   Come whispering by:
War's annals will cloud into night
   Ere their story die.

Thomas Hardy

* 'Thou art my battle axe and weapons of war: for with thee will I break in pieces the nations, and with thee will I destroy kingdoms', Jeremiah: 51:20.

Reconciliation

Word over all, beautiful as the sky,
Beautiful that war and all its deeds of carnage must in time be utterly lost,
That the hands of the sisters Death and Night incessantly softly wash again, and ever again, this
    soil'd world;
For my enemy is dead, a man divine as myself is dead,
I look where he lies white-faced and still in the coffin – I draw near,
Bend down and touch lightly with my lips the white face in the coffin.

Grass

Pile the bodies high at Austerlitz and Waterloo.
Shovel them under and let me work—
                I am the grass; I cover all.

And pile them high at Gettysburg
And pile them high at Ypres and Verdun.
Shovel them under and let me work.
Two years, ten years, and passengers ask the conductor:
                What place is this?
                Where are we now?

                I am the grass.
                Let me work.

Carl Sandburg

August 1914

What in our lives is burnt
In the fire of this?
The heart's dear granary?
The much we shall miss?

Three lives hath one life—
Iron, honey, gold.
The gold, the honey gone—
Left is the hard and cold.

Iron are our lives
Molten right through our youth.
A burnt space through ripe fields,
A fair mouth's broken tooth.

Letter to André Billy
9 April 1915

Gunner/Driver One (front-line)
Here I am and send you greetings
No no you're not seeing things
My Sector's number fifty-nine

I hear the whistle of
the the bird
beautiful bird of prey

I see far away
the cathedral

O   D
H   E
M   A
Y A R
N D R E
B I L L Y

Guillaume Apollinaire
Translated by Oliver Bernard

Harmonica

A tommy drops his harmonica in No Man's Land.
My dad like old Anaximenes breathes in and out
Through the holes and reeds and finds this melody.

Our souls are air. They hold us together. Listen.
A music-hall favourite lasts until the end of time.
My dad is playing it. His breath contains the world.

The wind is playing an orchestra of harmonicas.

'I know the truth — give up all other truths!'

I know the truth – give up all other truths!
No need for people anywhere on earth to struggle.
Look – it is evening, look, it is nearly night:
what do you speak of, poets, lovers, generals?

The wind is level now, the earth is wet with dew,
the storm of stars in the sky will turn to quiet.
And soon all of us will sleep under the earth, we
who never let each other sleep above it.

1915

Marina Tsvetaeva
Translated by Elaine Feinstein

Anthem
for Doomed Youth

What passing-bells for these who die as cattle?
   – Only the monstrous anger of the guns.
   Only the stuttering rifles' rapid rattle
Can patter out their hasty orisons.
No mockeries now for them; no prayers nor bells;
   Nor any voice of mourning save the choirs, –
The shrill demented choirs of wailing shells;
   And bugles calling for them from sad shires.

What candles may be held to speed them all?
   Not in the hands of boys, but in their eyes
Shall shine the holy glimmers of goodbyes.
   The pallor of girls' brows shall be their pall;
Their flowers the tenderness of patient minds,
And each slow dusk a drawing-down of blinds.

A Dead Statesman

from Epitaphs of the War 1914–18

I could not dig: I dared not rob:
Therefore I lied to please the mob.
Now all my lies are proved untrue
And I must face the men I slew.
What tale shall serve me here among
Mine angry and defrauded young?

Rudyard Kipling

Everyone Sang

Everyone suddenly burst out singing;
And I was filled with such delight
As prisoned birds must find in freedom,
Winging wildly across the white
Orchards and dark-green fields; on – on – and out of sight.

Everyone's voice was suddenly lifted;
And beauty came like the setting sun:
My heart was shaken with tears; and horror
Drifted away . . . O, but Everyone
Was a bird; and the song was wordless; the singing will never be done.

April 1919

The Long War

Less passionate the long war throws
its burning thorn about all men,
caught in one grief, we share one wound,
and cry one dialect of pain.

We have forgot who fired the house,
whose easy mischief spilt first blood,
under one raging roof we lie
the fault no longer understood.

But as our twisted arms embrace
the desert where our cities stood,
death's family likeness in each face
must show, at last, our brotherhood.

Laurie Lee

The Morning After (August 1945)

The fire left to itself might smoulder weeks.
Phone cables melt. Paint peels from off back
   gates.
Kitchen windows crack; the whole street reeks
of horsehair blazing. Still it celebrates.

Though people weep, their tears dry from the heat.
Faces flush with flame, beer, sheer relief
and such a sense of celebration in our street
for me it still means joy though banked with grief.

And that, now clouded, sense of public joy
with war-worn adults wild in their loud fling
has never come again since as a boy
I saw Leeds people dance and heard them sing.

There's still that dark, scorched circle on
   the road.
The morning after kids like me helped spray
hissing upholstery spring wire that still glowed
and cobbles boiling with black gas tar for VJ.

Return to Cornwall

I think no longer of the antique city
   Of Pompey and the red-haired Alexander.
The brilliant harbour, the wrecked light at Pharos,
   Are buried deep with Mediterranean plunder.

Here, by the Inney, nature has her city:
   (O the cypress trees of Mahomed Ali Square!)
The children build their harbour in the meadow
   And the crystal lark floats on the Cornish air.

Charles Causley

Accordionist

for André Kertesz

The accordionist is a blind intellectual
carrying an enormous typewriter whose keys
grow wings as the instrument expands into a tall
horizontal hat that collapses with a tubercular wheeze.

My century is a sad one of collapses.
The concertina of the chest; the tubular bells
of the high houses; the flattened ellipses
of our skulls that open like petals.

We are the poppies sprinkled along the field.
We are simple crosses dotted with blood.
Beware the sentiments concealed
in this short rhyme. Be wise. Be good.

The Visitor

In Spanish he whispers there is no time left.
It is the sound of scythes arcing in wheat,
the ache of some field song in Salvador.
The wind along the prison, cautious
as Francisco's hands on the inside, touching
the walls as he walks, it is his wife's breath
slipping into his cell each night while he
imagines his hand to be hers. It is a small country.

There is nothing one man will not do to another.

Carolyn Forché

Boy with Orange *(out of Kosovo)*

A boy holding an orange in his hands
Has crossed the border in uncertainty.

He stands there, stares with marble eyes at scenes
Too desolate for him to comprehend.

Now, in this globe he's clutching something safe,
A round assurance and a promised joy

No one shall take away. He cannot smile.
Behind him are the stones of babyhood.

Soon he will find a hand, perhaps, to hold,
Or a kind face, some comfort for a while.

Passing-Bells

That moment when the soldier's soul
slipped through his wounds, seeped
through the staunching fingers of his friend
then, like a shadow, slid across a field
to vanish, vanish, into textless air . . .
there would have been a bell in Perth,
Llandudno, Bradford, Winchester,
rung by a landlord in a sweating, singing pub
or by an altar-boy at Mass – in Stoke-on-Trent,
Leicester, Plymouth, Crewe, in Leeds, Stockport,
Littleworth – an ice-cream van jingling in a park;
a door pushed open to a jeweller's shop;
a songbird fluttering from a tinkling cat – in Ludlow,
Wolverhampton, Taunton, Hull – a parish church
chiming out the hour; the ringing end of school –

in Wigan, Caythorpe, Peterborough, Ipswich,
Aberdeen, King's Lynn, Malvern, Poole –
a deskbell in a quiet, dark hotel; bellringers' practice
heard by Sunday cricketers; the first of midnight's bells
at Hogmanay – in Huddersfield, Motherwell, Rhyl –
there would have been a bell in Chester,
Fife, Bridgend, Wells, Birkenhead, Newcastle,
in city and in town and countryside –
the crowded late night bus; a child's bicycle;
the old, familiar, clanking cow-bells of the cattle.

The Artist as 'Maker'

'I start with the visible'

'To see a World in a Grain of Sand'

To see a World in a Grain of Sand
And a Heaven in a Wild Flower,
Hold Infinity in the palm of your hand
And Eternity in an hour.

Mysteries

At night, I do not know who I am
when I dream, when I am sleeping.

Awakened, I hold my breath and listen:
a thumbnail scratches the other side of
the wall.

At midday, I enter a sunlit room
to observe the lamplight on for no reason.

I should know by now that few octaves can
be heard,
that a vision dies from being too long stared at;

that the whole of recorded history even
is but a little gossip in a great silence;

that a magnesium flash cannot illumine,
for one single moment, the invisible.

I do not complain. I start with the visible
and am startled by the visible.

In the microscope

Here too are dreaming landscapes,
lunar, derelict.
Here too are the masses,
tillers of the soil.
And cells, fighters
who lay down their lives
for a song.

Here too are cemeteries,
fame and snow.
And I hear murmuring,
the revolt of immense estates.

Miroslav Holub
Translated by Ian Milner

Fulcrum/Writing a World

'While I talk and the flies buzz,
a seagull catches a fish at the mouth of the Amazon,
a tree falls in the Adirondack wilderness,
a man sneezes in Germany,
a horse dies in Tattany, and twins are born in France.
What does that mean? Does the contemporaneity
of these events with one another,
and with a million others as disjointed,
form a rational bond between them,
and write them into anything
that resembles for us a world?'

Snow

The room was suddenly rich and the great bay-window was
Spawning snow and pink roses against it
Soundlessly collateral and incompatible:
World is suddener than we fancy it.

World is crazier and more of it than we think,
Incorrigibly plural. I peel and portion
A tangerine and spit the pips and feel
The drunkenness of things being various.

And the fire flames with a bubbling sound for world
Is more spiteful and gay than one supposes—
On the tongue on the eyes on the ears in the palms of one's hands—
There is more than glass between the snow and the huge roses.

Louis MacNeice

Blacksmith Shop

I liked the bellows operated by rope.
A hand or foot pedal – I don't remember which.
But that blowing, and the blazing of the fire!
And a piece of iron in the fire, held there by tongs,
Red, softened for the anvil,
Beaten with a hammer, bent into a horseshoe,
Thrown in a bucket of water, sizzle, steam.

And horses hitched to be shod,
Tossing their manes; and in the grass by the river
Plowshares, sledge runners, harrows waiting for repair.

At the entrance, my bare feet on the dirt floor,
Here, gusts of heat; at my back, white clouds.
I stare and stare. It seems I was called for this:
To glorify things just because they are.

Czesław Miłosz
Translated by Czesław Miłosz and Robert Hass

Birch Canoe

Red men embraced   my body's whiteness,
cutting into me   carved it free,
sewed it tight   with sinews taken
from lightfoot deer   who leaped this stream—
now in my ghost-skin   they glide over clouds
at home in the fish's   fallen heaven.

Carter Revard

Bowl

Give me a bowl, wide
and shallow. Patient
to light as a landscape open
to the whole weight
of a deepening sky.

Give me a bowl which turns
for ever on a curve
so gentle a child
could bear it and beasts
lap fearless at its low rim.

Miracle

A man, before going to bed, put his watch under his pillow.
Then he went to sleep. Outside the wind was blowing. You who know
the miraculous continuity of little motions, understand.
A man, his watch, the wind. Nothing else.

Yannis Ritsos
Translated by Rae Dalven

Vase

a word eradicates the world
a feather
drifts down

and yet, a bird's nest
in each of its fragments
preserves the whole

Yang Lian
Translated by John Cayley

Brooch

In memory of
Stephanie Macleod

They have their place, accessories:
earrings, the odd necklace,
gemstone bracelets . . .

and yet, it's from the soft inner depth
we work the brooch of our lives,
that jewelled keepsake set to outlast us.

Yours, it was a brooch ablaze –
the passion-crafted clasp,
the light chain to keep it safe;

others, now, will wear your brooch –
this jewel fashioned from a golden heart.
It will catch the sun. It will dazzle us.

Menna Elfyn
Translated by Elin ap Hywel

Bonnard

Colour of rooms. Pastel shades. Crowds. Torsos at ease in brilliant baths. And always, everywhere the light.

This is a way of creating the world again, of seeing differences, of piling shadow on shadow, of showing up distances, of bringing close, bringing close.

A way of furnishing too, of making yourself feel at home — and others. Pink, flame, coral, yellow, magenta — extreme colours for ordinary situations. This is a way to make a new world.

Then watch it. Let the colours dry, let the carpets collect a little dust. Let the walls peel gently, and people come, innocent, nude, eager for bed or bath.

They look newmade too, these bodies, newborn and innocent. Their flesh-tints fit the bright walls and floors and they take a bath as if entering the first stream, the first fountain.

Nothing Special

nothing special
boards paint
nails paste
paper string

mr artist
builds a world
not from atoms
but from remnants

forest of arden
from umbrella
ionian sea
from parkers quink

just as long as
his look is wise
just as long as
his hand is sure –

and presto the world –

hooks of flowers
on needles of grass
clouds of wire
drawn out by wind

Zbigniew Herbert
Translated by Czesław Miłosz and Peter Dale Scott

A Collector

The things I found
But they'll scatter them again
to the four winds
as soon as I am dead

Old gadgets
fossilised plants and shells
books broken dolls
coloured postcards

And all the words
I have found
my incomplete
my unsatisfied words

Erich Fried
Translated by Stuart Hood

Tin Roof

Wild harmattan winds whip you
but still you stay;
they spit dust all over your gleam
and twist your sharp cutting edges.
The rains come zinging mud
with their own tapping music
yet you remain
– my pride –
my very own tin roof.

Nii Ayikwei Parkes

Web

The deftest leave no trace: type, send, delete,
clear *history*. The world will never know.
Though a man might wonder, as he crossed the street
what it was that broke across his brow
or vanished on his tongue and left it sweet

Carving

Others can carve out
their space
in tombs and pyramids.
Our time cannot be trapped
in cages.
Nor hope, nor laughter.
We let the moment rise
like birds and planes and angels
to the sky.

Eternity is this.
Your breath on the window-pane,
living walls with shining eyes.
The surprise of spires,
uncompromising verticals. Knowing
we have been spared
to lift our faces up
for one more day,
into one more sunrise.

Imtiaz Dharker

In the Poem

To bring the picture the wall the wind
The flower the glass the shine on wood
And the cold chaste clearness of water
To the clean severe world of the poem

To save from death decay and ruin
The actual moment of vision and surprise
And keep in the real world
The real gesture of a hand touching the table.

Sophia de Mello Breyner
Translated by Ruth Fainlight

The Poet as Prophet

'I sing of a world reshaped'

I Sing of Change

'Sing on: somewhere at some new moon,
We'll learn that sleeping is not death,
Hearing the whole earth change its tune'
W. B. Yeats

I sing
of the beauty of Athens
without its slaves

Of a world free
of kings and queens
and other remnants
of an arbitrary past

Of earth
with no sharp north
or deep south
without blind curtains
or iron walls

Of the end
of warlords and armouries
and prisons of hate and fear

Of deserts treeing
and fruiting
after the quickening rains

Of the sun radiating ignorance
and stars informing
nights of unknowing

I sing of a world reshaped

Niyi Osundare

'And did those feet in ancient time'

And did those feet in ancient time
Walk upon England's mountains green?
And was the holy Lamb of God
On England's pleasant pastures seen?

And did the Countenance Divine
Shine forth upon our clouded hills?
And was Jerusalem builded here
Among these dark Satanic Mills?

Bring me my Bow of burning gold:
Bring me my Arrows of desire:
Bring me my Spear: O clouds unfold!
Bring me my Chariot of fire.

I will not cease from Mental Fight,
Nor shall my Sword sleep in my hand
Till we have built Jerusalem
In England's green & pleasant Land.

Ozymandias

I met a traveller from an antique land
Who said: Two vast and trunkless legs of stone
Stand in the desert . . . Near them, on the sand,
Half sunk, a shattered visage lies, whose frown,
And wrinkled lip, and sneer of cold command,
Tell that its sculptor well those passions read
Which yet survive, stamped on these lifeless things,
The hand that mocked them and the heart that fed;
And on the pedestal these words appear:
'My name is OZYMANDIAS, King of Kings:
Look on my works, ye Mighty, and despair!'
Nothing beside remains. Round the decay
Of that colossal wreck, boundless and bare
The lone and level sands stretch far away.

Percy Bysshe Shelley

Mama Dot

Born on a sunday
in the kingdom of Ashante

Sold on monday
into slavery

Ran away on tuesday
cause she born free

Lost a foot on wednesday
when they catch she

Worked all thursday
till her head grey

Dropped on friday
where they burned she

Freed on saturday
in a new century

Dream Boogie

Good morning, daddy!
Ain't you heard
The boogie-woogie rumble
Of a dream deferred?

Listen closely:
You'll hear their feet
Beating out and beating out a —

You think
It's a happy beat?

Listen to it closely:
Ain't you heard
something underneath
like a —

What did I say?

Sure,
I'm happy!
Take it away!

Hey, pop!
Re-bop!
Mop!

Y-e-a-h!

Langston Hughes

Season

Rust is ripeness, rust,
And the wilted corn-plume;
Pollen is mating-time when swallows
Weave a dance
Of feathered arrows
Thread corn-stalks in winged
Streaks of light. And, we loved to hear
Spliced phrases of the wind, to hear
Rasps in the field, where corn-leaves
Pierce like bamboo slivers.

Now, garnerers we
Awaiting rust on tassels, draw
Long shadows from the dusk, wreathe
Dry thatch in wood-smoke. Laden stalks
Ride the germ's decay – we await
The promise of the rust.

Free

Born free
to be caught
and fashioned
and shaped
and freed to wander
within
a caged dream
of tears

Merle Collins

Ourstory

Let us now praise women
with feet glass slippers wouldn't fit;

not the patient, nor even the embittered
ones who kept their place,

but awkward women, tenacious with truth,
whose elbows disposed of the impossible;

who split seams, who wouldn't wait,
take no, take sedatives;

who sang their own numbers, went uninsured,
knew best what they were missing.

Our misfit foremothers are joining forces
underground, their dusts mingling

breast-bone with scapula, forehead
with forehead. Their steady mass

bursts locks; lends a springing foot
to our vaulting into enormous rooms.

Optimistic Little Poem

Now and then it happens
that somebody shouts for help
and somebody else jumps in at once
and absolutely gratis.

Here in the thick of the grossest capitalism
round the corner comes the shining fire brigade
and extinguishes, or suddenly
there's silver in the beggar's hat.

Mornings the streets are full
of people hurrying here and there without
daggers in their hands, quite equably
after milk or radishes.

As though in a time of deepest peace.

A splendid sight.

Hans Magnus Enzensberger
Translated by David Constantine

Sometimes

Sometimes things don't go, after all,
from bad to worse. Some years, muscadel
faces down frost; green thrives; the crops don't fail,
sometimes a man aims high, and all goes well.

A people sometimes will step back from war;
elect an honest man; decide they care
enough, that they can't leave some stranger poor.
Some men become what they were born for.

Sometimes our best efforts do not go
amiss; sometimes we do as we meant to.
The sun will sometimes melt a field of sorrow
that seemed hard frozen: may it happen for you.

Lines from Hellas

The world's great age begins anew,
  The golden years return,
The earth doth like a snake renew
  Her winter weeds outworn:
Heaven smiles, and faiths and empires gleam,
Like wrecks of a dissolving dream.

Percy Bysshe Shelley

The Undertaking

The darkness lifts, imagine, in your lifetime.
There you are — cased in clean bark you drift
through weaving rushes, fields flooded with cotton.
You are free. The river films with lilies,
shrubs appear, shoots thicken into palm. And now
all fear gives way: the light
looks after you, you feel the waves' goodwill
as arms widen over the water; Love,

the key is turned. Extend yourself —
it is the Nile, the sun is shining,
everywhere you turn is luck.

Poetry: A Defence
'Poetry is with us from the start'

'Loving the rituals'

Loving the rituals that keep men close,
Nature created means for friends apart:

pen, paper, ink, the alphabet,
signs for the distant and disconsolate heart.

Palladas
Translated by Tony Harrison

Colmcille the Scribe

from the Irish, c. 11th century

My hand is cramped from penwork.
My quill has a tapered point.
Its bird-mouth issues a blue-dark
Beetle-sparkle of ink.

Wisdom keeps welling in streams
From my fine-drawn sallow hand:
Riverrun on the vellum
Of ink from green-skinned holly.

My small runny pen keeps going
Through books, through thick and thin,
To enrich the scholars' holdings –
Penwork that cramps my hand.

Colmcille: Sixth-century Irish saint, also known as St Columba, or 'Dove of the Church'.

Epilogue

I have crossed an ocean
I have lost my tongue
from the roots of the old one
a new one has sprung

Grace Nichols

The Language Issue

I place my hope on the water
in this little boat
of the language, the way a body might put
an infant

in a basket of intertwined
iris leaves,
its underside proofed
with bitumen and pitch,

then set the whole thing down amidst
the sedge
and bulrushes by the edge
of a river

only to have it borne hither and thither,
not knowing where it might end up;
in the lap, perhaps,
of some Pharaoh's daughter.

Nuala Ní Dhomhnaill
Translated by Paul Muldoon

From March '79

Tired of all who come with words, words but no language
I went to the snow-covered island.
The wild does not have words.
The unwritten pages spread themselves out in all directions!
I come across the marks of roe-deer's hooves in the snow.
Language but no words.

Tomas Tranströmer
Translated by John F. Deane

from **Poetry**

And it was at that age . . . Poetry arrived
in search of me. I don't know, I don't know where
it came from, from winter or a river.
I don't know how or when,
no, they were not voices, they were not
words, nor silence,
but from a street I was summoned,
from the branches of night,
abruptly from the others,
among violent fires
or returning alone,
there I was without a face
and it touched me.

Pablo Neruda
Translated by Alastair Reid

The Red Cockatoo

Sent as a present from Annam—
A red cockatoo.
Coloured like the peach-tree blossom,
Speaking with the speech of men.

And they did to it what is always done
To the learned and eloquent.
They took a cage with stout bars
And shut it up inside.

Po Chü-i
Translated by Arthur Waley

'You took away all the oceans and all the room'

You took away all the oceans and all the room.
You gave me my shoe-size in earth with bars around it.
Where did it get you? Nowhere.
You left me my lips, and they shape words, even in silence.

Osip Mandelstam
Translated by Clarence Brown and W. S. Merwin

Poetry

Who broke these mirrors
and tossed them
shard
by shard
among the branches?
And now . . .
shall we ask L'Akhdar to come and see?
Colours are all muddled up
and the image is entangled
with the thing
and the eyes burn.
L'Akhdar must gather these mirrors
on his palm
and match the pieces together
any way he likes
and preserve
the memory of the branch.

Saadi Youssef
Translated by Khaled Mattawa

Sonnet 65: 'Since brass, nor stone, nor earth, nor boundless sea'

Since brass, nor stone, nor earth, nor boundless sea,
But sad mortality o'ersways their power,
How with this rage shall beauty hold a plea,
Whose action is no stronger than a flower?
O how shall summer's honey breath hold out
Against the wrackful siege of batt'ring days,
When rocks impregnable are not so stout,
Nor gates of steel so strong, but Time decays?
O fearful meditation! where, alack,
Shall Time's best jewel from Time's chest lie hid?
Or what strong hand can hold his swift foot back?
Or who his spoil of beauty can forbid?
  O none, unless this miracle have might,
  That in black ink my love may still shine bright.

And Now Goodbye

To all those million verses in the world
I've added just a few.
They probably were no wiser than a cricket's chirrup.
I know. Forgive me.
I'm coming to the end.

They weren't even the first footmarks
in the lunar dust.
If at times they sparkled after all
it was not their light.
I loved this language.

And that which forces silent lips
to quiver
will make young lovers kiss
as they stroll through red-gilded fields
under a sunset
slower than in the tropics.

Poetry is with us from the start.
Like loving,
like hunger, like the plague, like war.
At times my verses were embarrassingly foolish.

But I make no excuse.
I believe that seeking beautiful words
is better
than killing and murdering.

Jaroslav Seifert

The Poet

Therefore he no more troubled the pool of silence.
But put on mask and cloak,
Strung a guitar
And moved among the folk.
Dancing they cried,
'Ah, how our sober islands
Are gay again, since this blind lyrical tramp
Invaded the Fair!'

Under the last dead lamp
When all the dancers and masks had gone inside
His cold stare
Returned to its true task, interrogation of silence.

George Mackay Brown

And Yet the Books

And yet the books will be there on the shelves, separate beings,
That appeared once, still wet
As shining chestnuts under a tree in autumn,
And, touched, coddled, began to live
In spite of fires on the horizon, castles blown up,
Tribes on the march, planets in motion.
'We are,' they said, even as their pages
Were being torn out, or a buzzing flame
Licked away their letters. So much more durable
Than we are, whose frail warmth
Cools down with memory, disperses, perishes.
I imagine the earth when I am no more:
Nothing happens, no loss, it's still a strange pageant,
Women's dresses, dewy lilacs, a song in the valley.
Yet the books will be there on the shelves, well born,
Derived from people, but also from radiance, heights.

Czesław Miłosz
Translated by Czesław Miłosz and Robert Hass

Acknowledgements

Every effort has been made to trace the copyright holders of the copyright material in this book and to provide correct details of copyright. Penguin regrets any oversight and, upon written notification, will rectify any omission in future reprints or editions. The editors and publisher gratefully acknowledge the following for permission to reprint copyright material:

Dannie Abse: 'Mysteries', from *New and Collected Poems* (Hutchinson, 2003). Reprinted by permission of United Agents.

Fleur Adcock: 'Immigrant', from *Poems 1960– 2000* (Bloodaxe Books, 2000). Reprinted by permission of Bloodaxe Books.

John Agard: 'Toussaint L'Ouverture Acknowledges Wordsworth's Sonnet "To Toussaint L'Ouverture"', from *Alternative Anthem: Selected Poems* (Bloodaxe Books, 2009). Reprinted by permission of Bloodaxe Books.

Moniza Alvi: 'Indian Cooking', from *Split World: Poems 1990–2005* (Bloodaxe Books, 2008). Reprinted by permission of Bloodaxe Books.

Anonymous: 'Anglo-Saxon Riddle', from *The Exeter Book Riddles*, translated by Kevin Crossley-Holland (Penguin, 1993), copyright © Kevin Crossley-Holland, 1993. Reprinted by permission of the translator, c/o Rogers, Coleridge and White Ltd, 20 Powis Mews, London, W11 1JN.

Guillaume Apollinaire: 'Letter to André Billy, 9 April 1915', from *Guillaume Apollinaire: Selected Poems*, translated by Oliver Bernard (Anvil Press Poetry, 1986; new edition 2004). Reprinted by permission of Anvil Press Poetry.

W. H. Auden: 'If I Could Tell You', from *Collected Poems*, revised edition (Faber & Faber, 2007), copyright 1945 by W. H. Auden, renewed. Reprinted by permission of Curtis Brown, Ltd.

Sebastian Barker: 'In the Heart of Hackney', from *Damnatio Memoriae: Erased from Memory*

(Enitharmon Press, 2004). Reprinted by permission of Enitharmon Press.

Matsuo Bashō: 'Autumn Evening', by Matsuo Bashō, translated by Kenneth Rexroth, from *One Hundred More Poems from the Japanese*, copyright © Kenneth Rexroth, 1976. Reprinted by permission of New Directions Publishing Corp.

Bei Dao: 'Winter Travels', from *Bei Dao: Landscape Over Zero*, translated by David Hinton and Yanbing Chen (Anvil Press Poetry, 1998). Reprinted by permission of Anvil Press Poetry.

Gerard Benson: 'Riddle', from *A Good Time* (Smith/Doorstop Books, 2010). Reprinted by permission of the author.

James Berry: 'Benediction', from *Hot Earth Cold Earth* (Bloodaxe Books, 1995). Reprinted by permission of Bloodaxe Books.

John Betjeman: 'City', from *Collected Poems*, copyright © The Estate of John Betjeman, 1955, 1958, 1962, 1964, 1968, 1970, 1979, 1981, 1982, 2001. Reprinted by permission of John Murray (Publishers) Ltd and the Estate of John Betjeman.

Sujata Bhatt: 'Finding India in Unexpected Places', from *Pure Lizard* (Carcanet Press, 2008). Reprinted by permission of Carcanet Press Ltd.

Earle Birney: 'giovanni caboto/john cabot', from *Rag & Bone Shop*, copyright © Earle Birney, 1971. Reprinted by permission of Wailan Low, Executor of the Estate of Earle Birney.

Elizabeth Bishop: 'One Art', from *Complete Poems 1927–1979*, copyright © Alice Helen Methfessel, 1979, 1983. Reprinted by permission of Farrar, Straus & Giroux, LLC.

Valerie Bloom: 'Sun a-shine, rain a-fall', from *Duppy Jamboree* (Cambridge University Press, 1992). Reprinted by permission of the author.

Eavan Boland: 'The Emigrant Irish', from *Collected Poems* (Carcanet Press, 1995). Reprinted by permission of Carcanet Press Ltd.

Yves Bonnefoy: 'Let a place be made', translated by Anthony Rudolf, translation copyright ©

Anthony Rudolf. Reprinted by permission of the translator and Mercure de France.

Kamau Brathwaite: 'Naima (for John Coltrane)', from *Jah Music* (Savacou Cooperative, 1986), copyright © Kamau Brathwaite, 1986. Reprinted by permission of the author.

Sophia de Mello Breyner: 'In the Poem' (*No Poema*), translated by Ruth Fainlight. Reprinted by permission of the translator.

George Mackay Brown: 'The Poet', from *Selected Poems 1954–1983*, copyright © George Mackay Brown, 1991. Reprinted by permission of John Murray (Publishers) Ltd.

John Burnside: 'A Private Life', from *Swimming in the Flood* (Jonathan Cape, 1995). Reprinted by permission of The Random House Group Ltd.

Ernesto Cardenal: 'On Lake Nicaragua', translated by Robert Pring-Mill, from *Apocalypse and Other Poems*, copyright © Ernesto Cardenal and Robert Pring-Mill, 1977. Reprinted by permission of New Directions Publishing Corp and Burns & Oates, an imprint of Bloomsbury Publishing Plc.

Charles Causley: 'Return to Cornwall', from *Collected Poems* (Macmillan, 1992). Reprinted by permission of David Higham Associates Ltd.

C. P. Cavafy: 'Longings', from *Collected Poems of C. P. Cavafy* (Chatto & Windus, 1990), translation © Edmund Keeley and Phillip Sherrard, 1990. Reprinted by permission of the translators, c/o Rogers, Coleridge and White Ltd, 20 Powis Mews, London, W11 1JN.

Paul Celan: 'Thread suns', from *Poems of Paul Celan*, translated by Michael Hamburger (Anvil Press Poetry 1988; 3rd edition 2007). Reprinted by permission of Anvil Press Poetry.

Cempulappeyanirar: 'What He Said', from *Cempulappeyanirar: Poems of Love and War*, translated by A. K. Ramanujan, translation copyright © A. K. Ramanujan, 1985. Reprinted by permission of Columbia University Press.

Faustin Charles: 'Viv', from *Children of the Morning: Selected Poems* (Peepal Tree Press, 2008). Reprinted by permission of Peepal Tree Press.

Judith Chernaik: 'Tortoise', from *The Carnival of the*

2000). Reprinted by permission of Bloodaxe Books.

Gavin Ewart: 'A 14-Year-Old Convalescent Cat in the Winter', from *Collected Poems 1980–1990* (Hutchinson, 1991), copyright © Gavin Ewart, 1991. Reprinted by permission of Margo Ewart.

Ruth Fainlight: 'Handbag', from *New and Collected Poems* (Bloodaxe Books, 2010). Reprinted by permission of the author.

Paul Farley: 'Monopoly', from *The Boy from the Chemist is Here to See You* (Picador, 1998), copyright © Paul Farley, 1998. Reprinted by permission of Picador, an imprint of Pan Macmillan.

James Fenton: 'Wind', from *The Memory of War and Children in Exile* (Penguin, 1983), copyright © James Fenton, 1983. Reprinted by permission of United Agents, on behalf of James Fenton.

Carolyn Forché: 'The Visitor', from *The Country Between Us*, copyright © Carolyn Forché, 1987. Reprinted by permission of William Morris Endeavor Entertainment, LLC, on behalf of the author.

Erich Fried: 'A Collector', from *100 Poems without a Country*, copyright © The Estate of Erich Fried, translation by and copyright © Stuart Hood, 1987, published by Calder Publications. Reprinted by permission of Alma Classics.

Robert Frost: 'Acquainted with the Night', from *The Poetry of Robert Frost*, edited by Edward Connery Latham (Jonathan Cape, 1971). Reprinted by permission of The Random House Group Ltd and Henry Holt.

John Fuller: 'Concerto for Double Bass', from *Selected Poems 1954–1982*, copyright © John Fuller, 1982. Reprinted by permission of the author.

Louise Glück: 'The Undertaking', from *The First Five Books of Poems* (Carcanet Press, 1997). Reprinted by permission of Carcanet Press Ltd.

Lorna Goodison: 'I Am Becoming My Mother', from *I Am Becoming My Mother* (New Beacon

Press, 1986). Reprinted by permission of New
Beacon Press.

Robert Graves: 'Love Without Hope', from
Complete Poems in One Volume, edited by Patrick
Quinn (Carcanet Press, 2000). Reprinted by
permission of Carcanet Press Ltd and A. P. Watt,
on behalf of the Robert Graves Copyright Trust.

Thom Gunn: 'The Reassurance', from *Collected
Poems* (Faber & Faber, 1993). Reprinted by
permission of Faber & Faber.

Choman Hardi: 'My children', from *Life for Us*
(Bloodaxe Books, 2004). Reprinted by permission
of Bloodaxe Books.

Tony Harrison: 'The Morning After (August
1945)', from *Collected Poems* (Penguin, 2007).
Reprinted by permission of Gordon Dickerson.

Seamus Heaney: 'The Rescue', from *Seeing Things*
(Faber & Faber, 1991), copyright © Seamus
Heaney, 1991; 'Colmcille the Scribe' (*Colum Cille
Cecinit*), from *Human Chain* (Faber & Faber,
2010), copyright © Seamus Heaney, 2010.
Reprinted by permission of Faber & Faber.

John Hegley: 'Into Rail', from *Beyond Our Kennel*
(Methuen, 1998). Reprinted by permission of
Methuen.

Cicely Herbert: 'Everything Changes, *after Brecht*';
Sappho, 'Two Fragments', translated by Cicely
Herbert. Reprinted by permission of Cicely
Herbert.

Zbigniew Herbert: 'Nothing Special', translated by
Peter Dale Scott, from *Zbigniew Herbert: Selected
Poems*, translated from the Polish by Czeslaw
Miłosz and Peter Dale Scott (Penguin, 1968).
Reprinted by permission of the translator.

Nazim Hikmet: 'Baku at Night', from *Poems
of Nazim Hikmet*, translated by Randy Blasing
and Mutlu Konuk. Translation copyright ©
Randy Blasing and Mutlu Konuk, 1994, 2002.
Reprinted by permission of Persea Books, Inc.,
New York.

Miroslav Holub: 'Spacetime', translated by David
Young and Dana Hábová, and 'In the microscope',
translated by Ian Milner, from *Miroslav Holub:
Poems Before and After: Collected English*

D. H. Lawrence: 'Piano', from *The Complete Poems of D. H. Lawrence* (Penguin, 1994). Reprinted by permission of Pollinger Limited and the Estate of Frieda Lawrence Ravagli.

Laurie Lee: 'The Long War', from *Selected Poems* (Penguin, 1985), copyright © Laurie Lee, 1985. Reprinted by permission of United Agents, on behalf of the Estate of Laurie Lee.

Denise Levertov: 'Living', from *Selected Poems* (New Directions, 1986), copyright © Denise Levertov, 1986. Reprinted by permission of Pollinger Limited and New Directions Publishing Corp.

Frances Leviston: 'Industrial', from *Public Dream* (2007), copyright © Frances Leviston, 2007. Reprinted by permission of Picador, an imprint of Pan Macmillan.

Li Bai: 'Listening to a Monk from Shu Playing the Lute', from *Three Chinese Poets,* translated by Vikram Seth. English translation copyright © Vikram Seth. Reprinted by permission of David Godwin Associates Ltd.

Michael Longley: 'Harmonica', from *Collected Poems* (Jonathan Cape, 2006). Reprinted by permission of The Random House Group Ltd.

Norman MacCaig: 'Stars and planets', and 'February – not everywhere', from *Collected Poems: A New Edition* (Polygon, 1990). Reprinted by permission of Polygon, an imprint of Birlinn Ltd (www.birlinn.co.uk).

Roger McGough: 'The Leader', from *Sky in the Pie* (Kestrel, 1983), copyright © Roger McGough, 1983. Reprinted by permission of Peters Fraser and Dunlop (www.petersfraserdunlop.com) on behalf of Roger McGough.

Jamie McKendrick: 'Out There', from *Dark Matter: Poems of Space*, copyright © Calouste Gulbenkian Foundation and Jamie McKendrick, 2008. Reprinted by permission of Calouste Gulbenkian Foundation and the author.

Louis MacNeice: 'Snow', and 'Coda', from *The Collected Poems of Louis MacNeice* (Faber &

Faber, 2007). Reprinted by permission of David Higham Associates Ltd.

Derek Mahon: 'Distances' (after Jaccottet), from *Words in the Air* (The Gallery Press, 1998); 'J. P. Donleavy's Dublin', from *New Collected Poems* (The Gallery Press, 2011). Reprinted by permission of The Gallery Press.

David Malouf: 'Thaw', from *Selected Poems 1959–89*, copyright © David Malouf, 1994. Reprinted by permission of the author, c/o Rogers, Coleridge and White Ltd, 20 Powis Mews, London, WII IJN.

Osip Mandelstam: 'You took away all the oceans', translated by W. S. Merwin and Clarence Brown, from *Selected Poems of Osip Mandelstam*. English translation copyright © W. S. Merwin, 1974. Reprinted by permission of the Wylie Agency (UK) Ltd.

Jack Mapanje: 'The Palm Trees at Chigawe', from *Of Chameleons and Gods* (Heinemann African Writers Series, 1981), copyright © Jack Mapanje, 1981. Reprinted by permission of the author.

Paula Meehan: 'Seed', from *The Man Who Was Marked by Winter* (The Gallery Press, 1991), copyright © Paula Meehan, 1991. Reprinted by permission of the author.

W. S. Merwin: 'Separation', from *The Moving Target* (Atheneum, 1963), copyright © W. S. Merwin, 1963. Reprinted by permission of the Wylie Agency (UK) Ltd; 'Rain Travel', from *Travels* (Alfred A. Knopf, 1993), copyright © W. S. Merwin, 1992. Reprinted by permission of Alfred A. Knopf, a division of Random House, Inc.

Edna St Vincent Millay: 'What lips my lips have kissed, and where, and why', from *Collected Poems*, copyright 1923, 1951 by Edna St Vincent Millay and Norma Millay Ellis. Reprinted by permission of The Permissions Company, Inc., on behalf of Holly Peppe, Literary Executor, The Millay Society, www.millay.org.

Czesław Miłosz: 'And Yet the Books', and 'Blacksmith Shop', translated by Czeslaw Miłosz and Robert Hass, from *New and Collected Poems 1931–2001* (Allen Lane, 2001), copyright ©

(Carcanet Press, 1991). Reprinted by permission of Carcanet Press Ltd.

Niyi Osundare: 'I Sing of Change', from *Selected Poems* (Heinemann, 1992), copyright © Niyi Osundare, 2002. Reprinted by permission of the author.

Palladas: 'Loving the rituals', translated by Tony Harrison, from *Tony Harrison: Collected Poems* (Penguin, 2007). Reprinted by permission of Gordon Dickerson.

Nii Ayikwei Parkes: 'Tin Roof', from *eyes of a boy, lips of a man* (Flipped Eye, 1999). Reprinted by permission of the author.

Don Paterson: 'Road', from *The Eyes* (Faber & Faber, 1999), copyright © Don Paterson, 1999. Reprinted by permission of Faber & Faber and the author, c/o Rogers, Coleridge and White Ltd, 20 Powis Mews, London, WII IJN; 'Web', from *Landing Light* (Faber & Faber, 2003), reprinted by permission of Faber & Faber.

Sylvia Plath: 'Child', from *Collected Poems* (Faber & Faber, 1981). Reprinted by permission of the Estate and Faber & Faber.

Po Chü-i: 'The Red Cockatoo', translated by Arthur Waley, from *Chinese Poems* (George Allen & Unwin, 1946). Reprinted by permission of the Arthur Waley Estate.

Vasko Popa: 'Belgrade', from *Vasko Popa: Complete Poems 1953–1987*, translated by Anne Pennington and Francis R. Jones (Anvil Press Poetry, 1997; enlarged edition 2011). Reprinted by permission of Anvil Press Poetry.

Peter Porter: 'Waiting for Rain in Devon', from *The Rest on the Flight: Selected Poems* (Picador, 2010), copyright © Peter Porter, 2010. Reprinted by permission of Picador, an imprint of Pan Macmillan.

Sheenagh Pugh: 'Sometimes', from *Selected Poems* (Seren, 1990). Reprinted by permission of Seren Books.

Kathleen Raine: 'Dreams', and 'Maire Macrae's Song', from *The Collected Poems of Kathleen Raine* (Golgonooza Press, 2000). Reprinted by

Owen Sheers: 'Swallows', from *Skirrid Hill* (Seren, 2005), copyright © Owen Sheers, 2005. Reprinted by permission of the author, c/o Rogers, Coleridge and White Ltd, 20 Powis Mews, London, WII IJN.

Iain Crichton Smith: 'The Exiles', from *Selected Poems* (Carcanet Press, 1985). Reprinted by permission of Carcanet Press Ltd.

Ken Smith: 'The bee dance', from *Shed: Poems 1980–2001* (Bloodaxe Books, 2002). Reprinted by permission of Bloodaxe Books.

Gary Snyder: 'Two Poems Written at Maple Bridge near Su-Chou', from *The Gary Snyder Reader* (Counterpoint Press, 1999), copyright © Gary Snyder, 1999. Reprinted by permission of Counterpoint Press.

Wole Soyinka: 'Season', from *Idanre and Other Poems* (Methuen, 1967). Reprinted by permission of Methuen.

Stephen Spender: 'To My Daughter', from *New Collected Poems* (Faber & Faber, 2004), copyright © Stephen Spender, 2004. Reprinted by permission of the Estate of Stephen Spender.

Wallace Stevens: 'Disillusionment of Ten O'Clock', from *The Collected Poems of Wallace Stevens* (Alfred A. Knopf, 1955), copyright 1954 by Wallace Stevens and renewed 1982 by Holly Stevens. Reprinted by permission of Faber & Faber and Alfred A. Knopf, a division of Random House, Inc.

Anne Stevenson: 'Ragwort', and 'It looks so simple from a distance', from *Poems 1955–2005* (Bloodaxe Books, 2005). Reprinted by permission of Bloodaxe Books.

Arthur Symons: 'A Tune', from *Collected Works of Arthur Symons* (Secker, 1924), copyright © Arthur Symons. Reprinted by permission of the Literary Estate of Arthur Symons.

George Szirtes: 'Accordionist', from *New and Collected Poems* (Bloodaxe Books, 2008), reprinted by permission of Bloodaxe Books.

Wislawa Szymborska: 'The Two Apes of Brueghel', translated by Grazyna Drabik with Sharon Olds,

Index of Poets

Index of First Lines

Wild harmattan winds whip you 240
'Will you walk a little faster?' said a whiting to a
    snail 183
Word over all, beautiful as the sky 207

Yellow/brown woman 114
You stood like women in green 48
You took away all the oceans and all the room 267
Your absence has gone through me 8
Your clear eye is the one absolutely beautiful
    thing 108

The Editors

Gerard Benson taught at the Central School of Speech and Drama for over twenty years. He was the author of ten poetry collections, for both adults and children, most recently his adult collection *A Good Time*, and he edited two Puffin anthologies. He was poet-in-residence at the Wordsworth Trust (the first Dove Cottage poet since Wordsworth himself), and gave many poetry recitals. In 2008 he became the City of Bradford's first Poet Laureate. His autobiographical *Memoirs of a Jobbing Poet* was published in 2014.

Judith Chernaik is the author of *The Lyrics of Shelley* and four novels, most recently *Mab's Daughters*, which was based on the lives of the Shelley circle and was published in Italian as *Le figlie di Mab*. She has published in the *TLS*, *Guardian*, *Musical Times*, *PN Review* and other journals, and has written features on Romantic poetry and music for the BBC. Her conversation piece about Mary Shelley and Mary Wollstonecraft, *The Two Marys*, has been widely performed in the UK and abroad. In 2002 she was awarded an OBE for services to literature.

Cicely Herbert is a writer, a performer and a member of the Barrow Poets. She has written several performance pieces, with music by Jim Parker; these include *Petticoat Lane*, for BBC TV, and two concert pieces commissioned by the Nash Ensemble, *Scenes from Victorian London* and *La Comédie Humaine*. Her radio play, *Yeats and Margot,* has been broadcast on BBC Radio 4, and her poems for children have been widely anthologised. Her book of poems, *In Hospital,* is dedicated 'To all who work for the National Health Service'.